GUY MARTIN

WITH ROD GREEN

HOW

BRITAIN

WORKED

Virgin BOOKS

2 4 6 8 10 9 7 5 3 1

First published in the United Kingdom in 2012 by Virgin Books, an imprint of
Ebury Publishing
A Random House Group Company

www.randomhouse.co.uk
Addresses for companies within The Random House Group Limited can be
found at www.randomhouse.co.uk/offices.htm

The Random House Group Limited Reg. No. 954009

A CIP catalogue record for this book is available from the British Library

The Random House Group Limited supports The Forest Stewardship Council
(FSC®), the leading international forest certification organisation. Our books
carrying the FSC label are printed on FSC® certified paper. FSC is the only forest
certification scheme endorsed by the leading environmental organisations,
including Greenpeace. Our paper procurement policy can be found at
www.randomhouse.co.uk/environment

Designed by Two Associates
Printed and bound in the UK by Butler Tanner and Dennis Ltd

ISBN: 9780753540848

To buy books by your favourite authors and register for offers,
visit www.randomhouse.co.uk

CONTENTS

INTRODUCTION

I'm a pretty lucky guy. I race motorcycles, which I love. I work as a truck mechanic, which I love. I race mountain bikes, which I adore. I also get to appear on the telly, and while I still don't really see myself a presenter, I'm slowly getting used to it. The thing that keeps me going back to it is that I get to meet so many people who are proper experts at what they do, and they don't mind sharing their knowledge with the likes of me – which really does make me feel extra fortunate.

The experts that I met while we were making the *How Britain Worked* TV series are all real enthusiasts who can talk about their own areas of expertise until the cows come home. Because they are so passionate about what they do, it's brilliant to spend time with them. I'm a good listener. You learn by listening to people with skills and talents and I learned a lot while we were filming.

It helped, of course, that I take a serious interest in any kind of machinery or engineering. I think we should all be proud of the things that clever and hard-working people in Britain have achieved – achievements in many cases that really did change the world. Britain's industrial heritage is something that we should all be proud of. Even though the ordinary working people – the backbone of the Industrial Revolution – were often treated appallingly, we should celebrate their skills and talents instead of just dwelling on the hardships they had to suffer. Having learned about how badly people were treated on the farms and in the factories, on the railways and in the coal mines, I know that we should never forget what they went through. At the same time, we should also never forget what they achieved.

That's one of the reasons why it was so fascinating for me to meet craftsmen who could, for example, make a wheel entirely out of wood. We all see and use wheels every day – on every truck, every car, every bus and every bike. How many of us could even start to imagine how to make one from scratch, using a few pieces of wood and some simple tools? That's more than just a skill, more even than a talent – it's artistry, an art that we shouldn't allow to die out.

Seeing how a wooden wheel could be built like that – and having a go myself – was an amazing experience. It was also pleasing to see how today's skilled workers use state-of-the-art technology to maintain and preserve the work of their predecessors. Time and again, I saw how modern methods worked hand-in-hand with traditional skills to reach a perfect end result. A Victorian

Learning how to
shorten a drive belt
with Tony at Gayle Mill
in Yorkshire.

engineer would be amazed by the sheer power of modern machines, let alone the robots and design computers used to create them.

Working with modern kit doesn't always mean that you're able to sit in the comfort of an air-conditioned office or workshop. Dangling underneath Llandudno Pier on a safety line, burning through Victorian ironwork with a cutting torch, was not a job that could be tackled with any degree of comfort at all. I wouldn't have missed that for the world, though. After all the time that I had spent chatting in front of a TV camera, that felt like a spot of proper hard graft. The fact that there was a slight element of danger thrown in made it all the better. Can I help it if I'm an adrenalin junkie?

Given that the TV series was about how the Industrial Revolution changed Britain, drawing people away from the countryside, creating huge cities and transforming the way that people worked and relaxed, I reckoned that we would be spending our time filming in the Midlands. I saw us in Birmingham, or maybe as far north as Manchester. That, after all, is the sort of area where British industry really took hold. Not a bit of it. We covered a heck of a lot of ground.

From Drumlanrig Castle in Scotland and Gayle Mill in North Yorkshire to Chatham Docks in Kent and the port of Brixham in Devon, we found people and organisations working to keep our industrial heritage alive. That was a real treat – finding so many who care so much about our history. The great American industrialist Henry Ford said that, 'History is more or less bunk. It's tradition. We don't want tradition. We want to live in the present and the only history that is worth a tinker's damn is the history we made today.' How wrong can you be? Old Henry was a real stick-in-the-mud. Despite what he said about making history, he strongly resisted making any changes or improvements to the Model T, the car that made his fortune in the early years of the twentieth century. He hadn't learned the lessons of the past. You can't stand still; you have to keep moving forward. The Victorians knew that. They were great innovators, developing new manufacturing techniques and machinery as fast as their constantly evolving technology would allow.

I think that keeping that sort of history alive helps us to see how far we have come, the mistakes we have made and how best we can press on into the future. The people that I spoke to when we were filming the TV series weren't stuck in a bygone age or trying to relive the past but they all had a healthy respect for the skills of the craftsmen who built modern Britain. I'm sure that every one of them could write a book about what they do – some already have done – and cramming all of the information that they could give us, along with all the stories they had to tell, into just six episodes on the telly was always going to be impossible.

Some of that information, some of what I learned and some of things that we didn't have time for in the TV series, have gone into this book. If you enjoy reading it as much as I enjoyed myself while we were filming, then maybe we will all have learned a bit more about the inventions, the industries and the people who helped to make Britain great.

THE
RAILWAYS

Nothing in the history of Britain affected the entire nation as much as the arrival of the railways. Nowadays we tend to take the rail network very much for granted, either because we use it so much, or because we never use it at all. In the south east of England, more than 860,000 people travel into London every morning by train. and we all know how much rail commuters love to moan about overcrowding, delays and high fares. It's fair enough to complain – when it all goes wrong you've got every right to feel hard done by. But what would it be like without the trains? That number of commuters could never all crowd on to London's roads – the capital of Britain would grind to a halt.

There are plenty of people outside the South East who also rely on the train to commute into town in Glasgow, Liverpool, Leeds, Manchester and Birmingham – 30,000 flood into Birmingham by train every morning – but for many it is easier to catch a bus at the street corner or step into a car. People who don't regularly travel by train (and I have to admit that I'm one of them) know that the rail network exists, but don't really see that it affects their lives a great deal. Yet without the railway network, we would never have developed into the world's first truly industrialised nation, and Britain today simply wouldn't work. Whether we as individuals take it for granted or not, Britain today still needs the rail network that was established 150 years ago.

THE WAY OF THE WAGON

Before the railways, goods that had to be transported in bulk went by sea around the coast and on rivers and canals inland. Lugging heavy goods such as timber or coal by horse and cart on Britain's roads, even where there were well-surfaced highways, was slow and expensive. The canal network, developed during the eighteenth century, was the most cost-effective way of transporting vast quantities of coal from the Midlands coalfields. Being able to deliver it in bulk meant that the cost of coal was slashed and that helped to encourage all sorts of industries to use coal for steam power. Getting coal from the pits to the canals, of course, often presented its own problems. One of the solutions was to extend the wooden board pathways that were used for hauling coal to the surface in the mines. The earliest tracks of wooden planks, laid to stop the wheels of heavily laden coal wagons getting bogged down on the wet, muddy floor of the mine, sometimes had a slot between the

An early illustration of a horse pulling a load of coal on a wagonway.

Do I look confused? Well, there was a lot to learn before I could drive our steam train!

NOT TO BE MOVED

timbers where a guide pole sticking out of the bottom of the wagon would fit to keep the wagon's wheels running on the planks. The 'slot car' system later gave way to wooden rails that guided the wheels.

The earliest of these 'wagonways' came long before the canal system, when they were used to move coal to river ports. Horses (or people if they would work cheaper) would be used to pull heavy trains of wagons on a slight downhill incline to the river. The slope made it easier for the horses to pull the huge loads: for the uphill journey on the way back, of course, the wagons were empty. One of the earliest examples was the Wollaton Wagonway, which was built just outside Nottingham in 1604. The wagonway was two miles long and cost about £170, which was a lot of money at the time. Even so, £85 per mile still seems cheap compared with the planned High Speed Two (HS2) rail link between London and Birmingham. The entire 335 miles of the new rail development, which will link with Manchester and Leeds, is estimated to cost £30 billion – that's more than £89 million per mile!

But £89 million per mile buys you a heck of a lot more than a wagonway. It gives you the ability to run trains at up to 250mph and cuts the journey time from London to Birminghan to under an hour. Even with a good downhill incline (which you're clearly not going to get all the way from London to Brimingham) and even if it was possible to do the journey non-stop without messing about changing horses, London to Birmingham on a wagonway would have taken at least a day and a half.

The wooden rails of the wagonways caused problems in that they wore out, or buckled or rotted, so they had to be replaced fairly frequently. They then tried 'capping' the wooden rails with iron, but that caused the wooden wagon wheels to wear out. The obvious solution was to have iron wheels, which ultimately ran on solid iron rails. The iron rail-and-wheel combination could carry far heavier loads than its wooden equivalent but eventually, from the time they were first laid at Derby Station in 1857, steel rails were accepted as the way forward.

ABSOLUTELY STEAMING!

Once the Industrial Revolution began to gather pace, the demand for coal became ever greater. Steam power was all the rage and coal was what everyone wanted to fire their boilers. By 1800, the firm of Boulton and Watt in Birmingham had built almost 500 steam engines, most of which were being used to power machinery in mills and factories. But if a steam engine could power machinery, turning flywheels that ran a shaft that used pulleys and gears to run all sorts of machines, then surely one could be used to haul goods on the wagonways? There were people who thought that a crazy idea, who thought that steam engines needed to be bolted down, that they would shake themselves to bits if they were made to move around and that a dangerous mobile furnace on wheels feeding a boiler that might blow itself apart at any moment was complete lunacy. There were others, however, who were clever enough, or daft enough, to give it a go.

Opposite: The notice was for the locomotive, not for me!

A steam engine that could operate on the railways, pulling greater loads at higher speeds, was something that several engineers were working hard to perfect. In 1801, Cornish engineer Richard Trevithick built a steam engine that would run not on rails but out on the public roads. He called it the *Puffing Devil* and tested it in London where the engine ran perfectly on its first outing but during further tests three days later, it broke down.

Trevithick and his cousin, who had been steering the beast, left the *Devil* under some shelter and went into a pub for lunch. While they were eating goose and quaffing a few ales, they let the boiler run dry and the *Puffing Devil* turned into a *Fiery Devil* by bursting into flames. The machine was destroyed, but it didn't put Trevithick off his experiments with steam. He had been around steam engines all of his life as his father was a mine 'captain', the most senior foreman in the mine, and the copper mines that were part of the landscape of Trevithick's childhood used steam engines to pump water out of the tunnels.

When Trevithick became a mining engineer, he designed steam engines that would use steam at higher pressures than had been used before, calculating that advances in the process for producing the wrought-iron boiler plates and pistons would make them strong enough to contain the pressure without blowing up (although one of his pumping engines did just that in Greenwich in 1803, killing four men).

Trevithick kept at it, adapting his designs so that he could use higher-pressure steam to provide more force, allowing him to get more work out of a smaller engine. That meant that he could start to think about making his engines portable – even self-propelled. In 1804, he adapted an engine that he had built at the Pen-y-Darren ironworks in Merthyr Tydfil. The engine was intended to power a heavy hammer used for crushing ore, but Trevithick altered it to make the engine drive itself along on wheels. The boss at the Pen-y-Darren works had bet one of his rich mine-owner friends 500 guineas (that's at least £25,000 in today's money – it must have been like Richard Branson having a bet with Alan Sugar) that Trevithick's steam engine could pull ten tons of iron ten miles along the Merthyr Tydfil Tramroad. In fact, Trevithick pulled ten tons of iron, five wagons and seventy men along the rails. The weight of the load, and the engine, broke some of the rails on which it was running and the Merthyr line returned to using lighter, horse-drawn wagons after Trevithick's experiment, but he had certainly started something, as well as winning his boss a tidy packet.

Trevithick wasn't the only one in the mining business to experiment with steam engines hauling wagons. In 1813, mining engineer William Hedley built an engine that he called *Puffing Billy* at the Wylam Colliery just outside Newcastle upon Tyne. The engine, and its sister, *Wylam Dilly*, were designed to haul coal on the wagonway that connected the colliery to the River Tyne at Lemington. The engines were rebuilt with four axles rather than two – eight wheels spreading the weight to avoid breaking the cast-iron wagonway plates – then changed again when more robust rails were laid. Messing around with steam engines in this way might seem like an expensive indulgence for the mine owner, Christopher Blackett, who funded Hedley's engine-building experiments, but the alternative was to use heavy horses and they were in short supply (as was horse fodder), due to so many of them being used by the military to fight Napoleon in Europe. *Puffing Billy* and *Wylam Dilly* turned out to be a sound investment, though, as they stayed in service for almost fifty years. *Puffing Billy* is now at the Science Museum in London and *Wylam Dilly* at the Royal Museum in Edinburgh.

BY GEORGE!

Hedley's engines were important not only because they proved that steam locomotives could have long, reliable lives, but also because they operated at the same colliery where a man called George Stephenson maintained the pumping engine. George's son, also called George, was a proper boy who was fascinated by all things mechanical – especially steam engines. By the time he was fifteen he was grafting with spanners and rags alongside his father and he soon moved on to a variety of machine-minding mining jobs. In 1811, he repaired the pumping engine at High Pit near Killingworth and did it so well that before long he was in charge of all the colliery engines in the area.

Opposite: William Hedley's 1813 locomotive, *Puffing Billy.*

Like Hedley, Stephenson built his own steam locomotives for use at various collieries, adapting and improving designs developed by others. When a group of mill owners, mine owners and other merchants decided that they needed a rail line to transport their goods to the River Tees, Stephenson persuaded them that it should use steam locomotives. In 1821 he was given the job of building the railway from Witton Park to Stockton-on-Tees via Darlington. It was twenty-six miles long – the longest in the world at that time.

Stephenson built several engines to run on the line, but the engine that pulled the first wagons on the Stockton and Darlington Railway (S&DR) was *Locomotion No. 1*. On its inaugural journey, *Locomotion No. 1* pulled thirty-three wagons carrying coal, flour and more than 600 passengers. All except the VIPs rode in open carriages; the posh folks sat in something that looked like a large garden shed. The train chugged along at about 12mph and when it arrived in Stockton there was a crowd of 40,000 people there to meet it.

Below: The first engine to be used on the Stockton and Darlington Railway was George Stephenson's *Locomotion No. 1.*

The Stephensons liked to keep their business in the family. George's eighteen-year-old son Robert (no, not another George) worked with his father on the S&DR. Father and son also became involved in building another new railway, this time the world's first intercity line between Liverpool and Manchester. The thirty-five-mile railway began in Liverpool with a tunnel more than a mile long underneath the city. The line included sixty-four

bridges and viaducts, as well as cuttings through solid rock and an iron bridge at Water Street in Manchester: it was a marvel of civil engineering. Although almost everyone believed that the line was a sound investment – 308 shareholders had parted with their hard-earned cash to own a slice of the Liverpool and Manchester Railway (L&MR) – not everyone was convinced that steam locomotives were the best power option. The S&DR, after all, didn't run entirely with steam engines: anyone who paid to use the track could transport wagonloads of goods pulled by horses if they so chose. Many colliery tracks also used cables, wound by stationary steam engines, to haul wagonloads of coal, a method that was especially effective on steep gradients where a steam locomotive's metal wheels couldn't grip the rails.

LAUNCHING THE ROCKET

To decide whether steam locomotives would be up to the job and, if so, what kind of steam engines should be used on the L&MR, a competition was held over several days at Rainhill in Lancashire on a stretch of the L&MR track, beginning on 6 October 1829. Ten locomotives entered the competition but on the first day only five actually competed. They had to make ten runs on the measured track, equivalent to the distance between Liverpool and Manchester. They had to pull a load three times their own weight; and they had to achieve a speed of at least 10mph (at that time the average speed of a locomotive on the S&DR was only 8mph).

The only engine successfully to complete the trials was George and Robert Stephenson's famous *Rocket*, which achieved an impressive top speed of 30mph, and an average speed of 12mph. The Stephensons won a prize of £500 and a contract to build locomotives for the L&MR. When the line opened in 1830, it was the first railway freight and passenger service with steam trains running to a set timetable, although on a couple of stretches of the track the trains were actually cable-hauled.

The success of the L&MR inspired a boom in the railway business in Britain. In the ten years up to 1835, Parliament sanctioned fifty-four new rail lines and by 1837 a further thirty-nine had been agreed. By 1845, there were 2,441 miles of railway carrying thirty million passengers annually, with proposals before Parliament for a further 9,500 miles of track the following year. Investors were clamouring to buy shares in railway companies. They saw it as a quick way to make a fortune and some families sank their entire life savings into the railways, but many of the new railways simply never transpired. A downturn in the economy and the fact that some of the supposed railway companies were fly-by-night operations that quickly went bust meant that a lot of people lost a lot of money in the investment frenzy that became known as 'Railway Mania'.

The sums involved in building a railway were pretty hefty. The L&MR had cost £637,000 – probably equivalent to about £53 million nowadays, although, as we've already seen, a mere £53 million wouldn't buy you much of a railway today!

A TOUCH OF CLASS

Nevertheless, by 1851 6,800 miles of track had been laid and over the next fifty years that total would more than treble, with the number of passengers carried soaring to 1,100 million annually. From her first journey in 1842, even Queen Victoria became a regular rail user, preferring the comfort and speed of the train to tiresome travel by horse and carriage. Not everyone travelled in such luxury, however, and passenger comfort had become a real issue on the railways. First-Class passengers travelled in some style, in carriages that were as well appointed as the horse-drawn carriages the railways were tempting them away from. Second-Class passengers had more basic coaches but were still travelling in relative comfort. Third-Class passengers, on the other hand, were lumped into the same sort of open wagons that were used for lugging coal or iron ore. If there was any kind of accident, and there were quite a few, Third-Class passengers could easily be flung out onto the track. On Christmas Eve in 1841 a train hauling three Third-Class passenger carriages and a variety of goods wagons was derailed by a landslide at the Sonning Cutting just outside Reading. The passengers were mainly stonemasons returning home for Christmas after working on the new Parliament building in London. Nine of them were killed and sixteen badly injured.

The safety of the newly mobile masses was at the heart of the Railways Act, which was introduced in 1844. This stipulated that at least one train should run on every line once a day in each direction, with adequate provision made for Third-Class passengers. Fares were set at a penny-a-mile, the passengers had to be in covered coaches, protected from the elements and the train was required to travel at at least 12mph. By setting out these rules,

Above opposite:
Queen Victoria's personal railway carriage allowed her to travel in comfort and style.

Below opposite:
I couldn't wait to have a go at driving 'our' engine, 5164.

the government hoped to encourage working-class people, the poorest in the country, to 'get on their bikes' and travel to where workers were urgently needed – in the factories and mills of the fast-growing industrial cities.

Not everyone was altogether chuffed about this. The Duke of Wellington reckoned that it was a mistake to let common people start to stray from their home territory and that the railways would encourage the poor and the criminal classes to come to London – he felt the capital had enough of those already! The middle class and more genteel passengers were also none too pleased at having to share their station platforms with the great unwashed. But once it started, there was no stopping the transport revolution. Some rail companies, which had always seen passengers as coming second to their main business of transporting goods in bulk, quickly realised that passenger transport was bringing in twice as much revenue as freight. Rather than invest in expensive new rolling stock for Third Class, however, they simply did away with Second Class, rebadging the Second-Class carriages as Third Class. Regular Second-Class passengers were horrified at first, seeing this as an affront to their social status, but by all accounts they soon got used to the situation. They had little choice. People were now coming to rely on the railways rather than seeing them as an entertaining novelty.

The trains themselves improved enormously as the rail network expanded across the country. The first toilets appeared on trains in the 1860s (most people at that time didn't even have one indoors at home), there were sleeping cars on longer routes by 1873 and you could tuck into a proper meal in a dining car by 1879. By the end of the nineteenth century, trains were travelling the length and breadth of the country at speeds of up to 70mph. The rail network boasted almost 40,000 tunnels and bridges, including the great bridges over the River Tay, the Forth and the Severn.

THE MEN WHO REALLY BUILT THE RAILWAYS

The rail network had been laid at an unbelievable pace, and that was down to a group of remarkable men: surveyors and engineers like Isambard Kingdom Brunel, who planned and designed the Great Western Railway (GWR – people called it God's Wonderful Railway) linking London to Bristol; and Robert Stephenson who engineered the London and Birmingham Railway. Brunel, Stephenson and others are remembered as the architects of the railways, but the men who actually built the railways were the 'navvies'.

The word 'navvy' is a short form of the word 'navigator' and the navigators were the workmen who dug or 'navigated' the canal system in the eighteenth century. In the nineteenth century, navvies were the men working on the railways. These were not educated men like the surveyors, architects and engineers. They were raw, strong blokes who worked with picks, shovels and wheelbarrows. Power tools and mechanical diggers were still in their infancy and were not as reliable as the brute force of the navvies. What the navvies

Opposite: Learning what all of 5164's levers, taps and gauges are for.

STEPHENSON TEACHING THE NAVVIES.

achieved is the most easily overlooked accomplishment of the railway boom. You can't run a railway without rails – it's in the name, after all – but the rails are the part of the railway that most of us really do take for granted. They're not glamorous like a steam locomotive or pretty like a country station, but they do have an elegant beauty all of their own. It's the never-ending symmetry, the perfect curves and the parallel lines that sweep off into the distance. I don't suppose everybody appreciates that, but I get it, and I know there are plenty of others who do, too. Unlike the steam locomotives and so many of the pretty country stations, we are still using the basic tracks that the navvies laid when we travel by train today. Their hard graft is there for all to see.

The work rate of the navvies was mind blowing. Every man would shovel 20 tons of muck or ballast a day. When they first started out as navvies, they might not be physically strong enough to keep up and would work only half a day so that they didn't drop from exhaustion. It could take up to a year before a man regularly took on full shifts as a navvy – it was a dangerous enough job without working yourself to death. At least three men were killed every day building the railways and one of the most notorious casualty sites was at the Woodhead Tunnels that were dug through the Pennines between 1837 and 1852 to link Manchester and Sheffield. At one time there were 1,500 men working on the three-mile-long tunnels and when a doctor, Henry Pomfret, visited Woodhead he reported that he had discovered twenty-three cases of compound fractures, seventy-four simple fractures, over a hundred cases of serious burns from blasting – and thirty-two deaths. On top of this, the navvies lived in a shanty town out on the moors and an outbreak of cholera in 1849 caused a further twenty-eight deaths. It was said that a man had more chance of being killed working on the Woodhead Tunnels than he did at the Battle of Waterloo.

It was normal for the navvies to live in a collection of ramshackle huts close to where they were working. These shanty towns followed the rail lines and the navvies slept twenty to a shed. They paid a penny-a-night for a bed and a penny-a-week to sleep on the floor, and that came out of a wage that might be five shillings a day. For those of you, like me, who know only our modern decimal currency, there were twelve pennies in a shilling and twenty shillings in a pound. That meant that, in the middle of the nineteenth century, a navvy was reasonably well paid. Yet no one, except perhaps the local publicans, wanted them coming into their towns and villages to spend their wages. When the railway workings approached a town and the navvies were in the area, police leave was cancelled. Navvies consumed two pounds of beef, two loaves of bread and ten pints of beer a day. It wasn't exactly an athlete's diet, but it was certainly the kind of high carbohydrate intake that they needed to do the work that they did. If they went on what they called a 'randy' – a drinking spree that might last a couple of days – the beer intake went through the roof, work on the railway ground to a halt and the local town descended into a shambles of drunkenness and brawling.

Opposite: The navvies were a rough-and-ready army of men, but the railway lines they built are still in use today.

To us nowadays, that sort of behaviour is simply unacceptable, but you can understand why the navvies notoriously acted this way. There were 250,000 of them working on the tracks at the height of the railway boom – more men than there were in the army and the navy combined – and they were just as expendable as the lowliest infantryman. The railway owners didn't care how many men died: they just wanted their railway built, and built as quickly as possible. Because the navvies never knew when their number would be up, they treated every day as if it were their last. At the end of their gruelling shift, they were down the pub, if they could get to one, making the most of the fact that they had survived another day working on the railway. The pub, as it happened, might well be where they gathered to collect their company wages. As likely as not, the pub would be also owned by the same company and happily accepted the men's wages back over the bar!

For all the drinking, the navvies' work rate was legendary. European railway companies tried to tempt British navvies abroad by offering them up to twice the wages they could earn at home. Their skills were in great demand: the navvies didn't just dig, they also knew about tunnelling, how to prop up the roof, how best to blast or dig different kinds of rock or soil and how to lay the rails sweet and level.

TIME TO GET MY HANDS DIRTY

I joined a track-laying gang on the Severn Valley Railway to get a taste of at least part of what a navvy's job was like. The Severn Valley Railway is a hugely popular heritage route that operates sixteen miles of track in Shropshire and Worcestershire following the valley between Bridgnorth and Kidderminster. This was where I really learned about the railways, working with some real enthusiasts who put an enormous amount of work into preserving and restoring the line, the rolling stock and the stations. They've turned the railway into a little slice of the past. When I was there they also arranged for the sun to shine, which made it all the more magical.

I was to spend quite a bit of time with the people who run the Severn Valley Railway and worked for a whole day with the track gang relaying a section of track to remove a hump. This was proper hard graft – hammering, lifting, carrying and digging. Each length of rail weighs one ton and manoeuvring it into place was no easy task. Then we had a train come past while we were working: a klaxon sounded and everyone cleared off the track sharpish. I picked up the tools I was using, gave the rail one last knock and then heard someone shouting, 'Get off the track, Guy!' I thought that I had all the time in the world, but it was explained to me that a train can't stop or swerve to avoid me if I'm on the track in front of it. All it would take would be for me to stumble or trip, maybe a slight panic wondering which way to jump, and they'd be picking up bits of me for hundreds of yards down the line. A navvy didn't only have to worry about being blown up, buried, crushed or killed by cholera – he could easily be run over as well. Lesson learned.

A track gang
at work on the Severn
Valley Railway.

Working with the track gang was hard graft but I enjoyed it, and when I'm
enjoying myself like that I do sometimes tend to natter on a bit. I had a radio
microphone attached so that I could describe what we were doing for the
film crew, but it's easy to forget that you're wired for sound. Levering rails
into place and hammering in the retaining clips, I said something along the
lines of, 'By heck, much more of this and I'll have muscles on me shit!' It was
then that the TV director's voice boomed out, 'Guy! Could you please use a
phrase that's a little less colourful?'

It took fifteen of us in the track gang all morning to lay about 60 feet of track.
Back in 1869, eight Irish navvies went over to America and laid ten miles of
track in twenty hours. The Irishmen had a few Chinese labourers working
for them, but that's still some going. I don't think that our track gang could
keep up with the hardcore navvies of the nineteenth century. In the novel *To
Kill A Mockingbird*, the lawyer Atticus Finch says, 'Never judge a man until
you have walked a mile in his shoes.' I don't think I came close to walking a
mile in a navvy's shoes – a yard or so maybe.

Nothing beats the view from the footplate of a steam locomotive.

The people at the Severn Valley Railway were able to show me what it was like for all sorts of workers on the railways, not just the navvies. In 1851, there were fifty-five women and around 54,000 men working on the railways. How many is that really? Well, you wouldn't get them all in a phone box, but neither would they fill Wembley Stadium. Ten years later, there were enough men (and 160 women) to fill Wembley – and the capacity there is 90,000. These weren't navvies, but they were railway workers. So what were their jobs?

GOING LOCO

If you're building a railway, once you've got your tracks in place, the next thing you need is a steam locomotive. Dozens of companies throughout Britain built steam locomotives, from Nielson and Company in Glasgow to Peckett and Sons in Bristol, although the different railway companies eventually had their own workshops building, maintaining and repairing their locos. Today, the Severn Valley Railway (SVR) has more than two dozen such locomotives, some of which are on display and some of which are undergoing restoration: they generally have about six locos in full working order.

The Severn Valley Railway offered me the chance to help carry out some of the restoration and repair work required to put one of these locomotives back on the rails.

At Bridgnorth, where the SVR's main locomotive workshop is, I was introduced to 5164 – no fancy name or anything, just a number – a 140-ton legacy of the steam age. It was every small boy's dream, to have a steam loco to play with, but she was looking a bit sorry for herself when I first saw her. I felt really proud that I was going to help lick her back into shape. 5164 is a Large Prairie Class or GWR 5101 class engine that was the backbone of God's Wonderful Railway, used on local passenger services all over the network. More than 200 of them were produced at GWR's Swindon engine works between 1903 and 1949 and they stayed in service until 1965. It's a real novelty when we see a steam engine on a railway line nowadays, isn't it? It's hard to believe that up to the end of the 1960s, almost every train was pulled by a steam locomotive. Steam powered the railways for over 140 years.

In order that I could understand all of the jobs that were carried out on an everyday basis when 5164 was in service, I started out on the bottom rung of the 'engine' ladder, as an engine cleaner. The engine cleaners were the lowest of the low and they had the dirtiest of jobs. One of the lads at Bridgnorth – everyone called him 'Monkey' – showed me the ropes. We had to flush out all of the gunge that had accumulated in the steam pipes in the boiler and in the air tubes that run through the boiler. It's a regular maintenance job and would have been done after the engine had come out of service and after it had cooled down. You have to wash out all the muck and limescale – the same sort of stuff you get bunging up your kettle. This was the donkey work.

The sun shone on 5164 when we took her on her first outing after her overhaul.

Putting my wrought-iron shovel to work aboard 5164.

It's dirty work. The lads doing this in the 1860s, when navvies were earning five shillings a day, were on just ten shillings a week and if you didn't do it properly, you were sacked. A train would come in at night and had to be made ready to go back out in the morning again. The engine cleaners would work a twelve-hour shift and during the winter, when the temperatures dropped, the metal parts of the train got so cold that in the morning they would find lads frozen to the train. It gets cold in my garage when I'm working on trucks but I've never yet been found frozen to one in the morning. We don't know we're born with our cushy jobs nowadays, do we?

We used a petrol-soaked rag torch on the end of a wire to inspect the waterways inside the boiler, poking it through inspection holes and peering in to look for blockages. I was shown how to use a little hand mirror so that I could check areas that I couldn't see directly, and was surprised at how little corrosion there was. On the inside, most of the pipework looked like the day it was put in. It turned out I had only been playing at engine cleaning so far. Monkey then showed me how to crawl inside the actual firebox, where they shovel in the coal, and use a 'stay testing hammer' to bash all the stays or rivets, and check that they are sound. The boiler on an engine like 5164 has two metal skins to contain the steam pressure and these are riveted together with hundreds of rivets. When you give the rivet a bash, there is a distinctly different, flatter, lower ring to a broken rivet. You are allowed just two broken rivets in a firebox and 5164 only needed a couple to be replaced before her boiler was passed fit for service.

It is a very tight squeeze, easing yourself into the firebox feet first, but there's a surprising amount of space once you are inside: not quite enough room to swing a cat, but more space than you might think. When you see coal being shovelled in through the hole, you might think that the firebox is a bit like a domestic fireplace. In fact, it's a lot bigger than that. This isn't just a simple coal fire; it's so big that it takes three or four hours to get going. It's only when you are inside the firebox that you really appreciate how a steam engine actually works. The heat from the fire passes along a network of air tubes, with the loco's funnel drawing the heat just like the chimney on a house draws smoke and heat up the chimney. The air tubes pass through a tank that is full of water, turning the water to steam.

The first steam trains had only one heater tube, but they soon found that more tubes worked better; 5164 has dozens of them. This creates more surface area where the hot metal of the tubes is in contact with the water, which heats the water more efficiently. Naturally, all of these tubes need to be cleaned out as well. Monkey and I cleaned out the heating tubes by blasting air through them. Most of the muck and soot from inside the tubes was blasted straight back out at us. We couldn't see a thing in there and could hardly breathe, the air was so thick with soot. Monkey had been on that job for nearly a week. I don't mind getting dirty – in fact, I'm famous for enjoying

Basking in the glow from a well-stoked boiler. I was never cold when working on the footplate.

getting filthy doing a bit of hard graft – but even I didn't envy Monkey that job. We had an electric lamp with us when we were working in the firebox but a lad doing this job in the nineteenth century would have been working by candlelight; and he would have worked a minimum twelve-hour shift. One fourteen-year-old GWR engine cleaner, John Harris, having worked three twelve-hour shifts in a row, fell asleep in the firebox. When a stoker came to fire up the boiler, he didn't notice poor John and tipped a shovel of hot, glowing coals all over him. John died from his burns. Sends a shiver down your spine, doesn't it?

Despite such tragedies, there was no shortage of youngsters who wanted to become engine cleaners. It was seen as the first stage on the promotion ladder that might lead you to one day becoming an engine driver, if you worked hard. Not that you had much choice about working hard, mind. An engine cleaner might have to start a shift at 3.00 a.m. That meant getting up at 1.30 a.m., and a 'knocker upper' was employed to come to your house and bang on the door until he got an answer. The railway companies liked their staff to live close to where they worked so that they could be called upon to work extra shifts whenever they were needed. If you refused to do the extra shifts, you could be fined.

If the engine cleaner kept his nose as clean as the engine, and learned enough about other people's jobs as well as the railway regulations to pass an examination, then he would be promoted to passed cleaner. That meant he could be relied upon to stoke the boiler as well as clean it. He could then look forward to progressing through at least three levels as a fireman before he had any chance of becoming a driver. All of that might take twenty-five years and if, after suffering all those years of muck and soot and grease and oil, his eyes were not deemed 100 per cent perfect, he would never make it as an engine driver. A driver not only had to be an expert on how his engine worked, and be able to maintain it, he also had to pass stringent eyesight and colour recognition tests. This was to ensure he could identify signals correctly at a distance, part of the increasing safety measures being introduced to cut accidents on the ever-busier railways. By 1900, drivers had to pass not only an eyesight test but also an annual medical exam.

The driver was the senior man on the footplate and demanded complete respect. The class divisions in British society most definitely extended to the workplace, and status was everything. If you had earned your place on a certain rung of the ladder, you expected those below you to show you proper respect, just as you, in turn, deferred to those higher up the ladder. A fully qualified driver was one of the gods of the engine shed. Fortunately, I wouldn't have to wait twenty-five years for my chance to drive a locomotive.

Yet another little job for the oil can.

A BIT OF A WOBBLE

Before I could take my place on the footplate, there were various parts that had to be fabricated to get 5164 running. In the Bridgnorth workshop they have a fine selection of engineering tools and I had the chance to help turn out a few bits and pieces. I will admit that I sometimes get more nervous starting up a machining tool than I do sitting on a start line before a motorcycle race. One of the lads minding a machine in the workshop where a part was being milled was sitting reading a book while the machine did its job. I, however, couldn't take my eyes off the job while I was doing it. Even though I knew that the machine was set right and doing the job, even though I'm a mechanic and knew that it wasn't about to go wrong, I just couldn't bear the thought of it not turning out right.

I became an apprentice to an apprentice when they discovered that 5164 had a spot of wheel wobble. A slight wobble might not seem to matter much on a machine of this size but, when she's running at speed, it's the sort of thing that can cause vibrations that can do real damage. I helped to manhandle two tons of wheel and axle into position in the workshop so that we could use a micrometer (the biggest one I'd ever seen) to measure the thickness of the axle and find out what was going on. This was proper muck-and-grease heavy-duty engineering. I was told that measuring the axle had to be done accurately because, just like on my motorbike, something that isn't right is going to break. Vibrations could start to shake the loco apart. Bearings would start to run hot and could seize up.

According to the micrometer there was a variance of only five 'thou' (five thousandths of an inch, or 0.2mm) over the entire length of the axle. That is quite remarkable given that the axle was machined a hundred years ago, by men who had no computer-aided precision machines to help them: all they had to go on were careful measurements and a skilful eye. When it was new, there would have been no discrepancy – the axle would have been of uniform thickness over its entire length. The standards may have been set by fancy design engineers like Brunel, but the skilled craftsmen who created things like the train axle were true engineers, masters of their craft. Have you ever seen pictures of someone like Stephenson standing next to a lathe? I haven't.

Five 'thou' was within tolerance, so the wobble had to be coming from somewhere else. The problem was traced to a crank pin, the bit that sticks out from the wheel where the crank arms are attached. Its bearing was worn and a new one had to be fabricated. To make the new, perfectly round, bearing, it had to be cast and I had to learn about the old-fashioned technique of white metalling. This was when I was made an apprentice to an apprentice, as seventeen-year-old Mark showed me how it was done.

We had a metal mould that we heated using a blowtorch so that the bearing wouldn't stick to it or shrink onto it when it was set. Once the mould was good

New bearings solved the problem of 5164's slight wheel wobble.

Levelling the coal in the bunker behind 5164's cab.

and hot, we poured in a cocktail of molten metal: a mixture of tin, copper, lead and an element called antimony. This took about twenty minutes to set into the round, disc-with-a-hole-in-the-middle bearing. The outside dimensions of the set bearing were correct for it to fit into the hole at the end of the crank arm, but it was a tight squeeze and we used an enormous press to force it in. Once it was tightly in there, we could start machining the inner surface of the bearing.

The machining process was carried out under the watchful eye of twenty-two-year-old Will. We needed the bearing to have an inner diameter of four inches, 408 'thou' for a perfect fit, and could afford a tolerance of about a thousandth of an inch. The crank arm with the bearing in place was set on another machine, carefully aligned so that the cutter could scrape the tiniest of fractions off the surface. Will showed me how to cut, measure, cut and measure until finally he reckoned it was done. The final measurement I took was four inches, 407 'thou'. Pretty much spot on. I don't know many twenty-two-year-olds who could do that, but Will is a craftsman who truly loves his job. He told me that if he was offered the choice between a job worth hundreds of thousands of pounds or told he could carry on working on the trains, he'd choose the trains every time. That's dedication for you. Needless to say, when we took the bearing out and tried it on the crank pin on the loco, with a little lubrication, it fitted like a glove.

THE ACE OF SPADES

My next step towards becoming an engine driver was to work as a fireman. I was going to need a shovel, and the shovel I wanted had to be made the way it might have been done in the nineteenth century. That meant I could get to grips with one of the revolutionary materials of the Industrial Revolution – wrought iron.

Wrought iron is different from cast iron in a number of ways, including how it is made. Cast iron is poured into a mould and allowed to cool and harden. When wrought iron is produced in its molten form, it is allowed to cool only so far. Because it has less carbon in it than cast iron, it is more malleable. It can be rolled into bars or sheets or stamped in its soft state. It can be worked, which is what 'wrought' actually means. Because it has fewer carbon 'impurities', a cold wrought-iron bar can also be reheated and worked into shape, something that you can't really do with a cast-iron bar. Wrought iron was used instead of cast iron for making a multitude of things from simple nails and railway rails to horseshoes and ships. They made the Eiffel Tower in Paris out of wrought iron. If it was good enough for what was then the world's tallest building, it was good enough for my shovel!

I went to see a man called Mike Wilkins, who gave up a desk job years ago to learn the blacksmith's trade and make things out of metal. Mike can turn out delicate ironwork made to look like flowers or small trees and ornamental creations that serve as garden gates. So showing me how to make a shovel was all in a day's work. First we cut a wrought-iron bar to size to make the shaft of the shovel. Using a hacksaw on a piece of metal held in a clamp, you have to get your stance right to work the hacksaw. My first foreman told me that you've got it right if you can feel your balls squeezed between your legs: I have no idea how he would have explained it to a female apprentice!

There was a furnace in Mike's workshop – a proper blacksmith's furnace where we could just nestle the wrought iron in amongst the coals to heat it up. Again we were using shedloads of coal or coke in the furnace: it really was what fuelled the Industrial Revolution. I put the end of the shaft into the coals to heat it so that it could be looped round to form a handle. It took just a few seconds to heat the metal to 1,000 degrees Celsius – the temperature at which it could be worked without damaging its internal structure, and snapping or shattering it.

When I picked the iron bar out of the bed of coal, the end was glowing red-hot. I had to swing round and lay it on the curved end of the anvil. It was a heavy old beast: you wouldn't want that landing on your foot! It was then a question of bashing the red-hot end to bend it over the curved surface of the anvil and create the handle loop. Mike had a few things to say about my hammering technique and reckoned I was being too gentle. He seemed to think that I was more interested in making a nice rhythmic sound than bending the metal, but I got there in the end.

Once the loop was created, we then had to make a fire weld to close the end of the loop. This meant superheating the metal to 1,400 degrees Celsius, until its surface actually starts to melt, and then melding the end to the shaft with a few mighty wallops. Or at least, that's what I thought. Mike explained to me that I had to judge my hammer blows like I was swatting a fly, so my 'softly-softly' approach was now going to work just fine. Even an experienced blacksmith, apparently, can get a fire weld wrong. If you hit it too many times and lose too much metal (bits fly off the molten surface every time you whack it) the handle could be too weak to use.

Bashing it about knocked our loop handle out of shape. We were able to force it back into a nice curve again by using a cone anvil, forcing the misshapen loop down over the ever-widening cone with our trusty hammer in order to coax the loop back into shape. While the handle was cooling down (I wouldn't fancy picking it up at 1,400 degrees!), Mike and I heated and shaped a sheet of wrought iron for the blade of the shovel.

We hammered the flat sheet into shape on a metal bed that was a bit like an oversized ashtray. I could move the blade around and bash it with my hammer to make it take on the curves of the shovel. We then had to work on attaching the end of the shaft to the blade.

Filling up with water to make sure that 5164 doesn't run out of puff.

To do this, we had to stick the end in the furnace and heat it up, then hammer it flat so that it could be split with the treadle hammer. This was a fine piece of kit that stood upright, taller than a man, with a kick-handle that you pushed down with your foot. Levers and counterbalances then brought a mighty hammerhead down on a striking plate. Sitting on the striking plate was the flattened end of our shovel shaft, and carefully poised on top of that was a heavy axe blade. The treadle hammer drove the axe head straight through the red-hot shaft, creating a cleft in the bottom. Once the shaft had been split, we clamped it in a vice. I was then able to use the axe head, hammering it into the cleft to make the split wider. When you see how solid this piece of metalwork ended up, it's hard to believe that I was able to work it almost like a piece of wood (albeit a very, very hot piece of wood).

The shaft now had two prongs at the end that, when we heated them in the furnace, we were able to puncture with holes that would take rivets. We didn't drill the holes, we just hammered a punch through the hot metal. Drilling, in fact, would have weakened the ends of the shaft. You drill metal out to create a hole. Punching the hole through just pushed the hot metal out of the way so that it flowed around the hole. You don't lose any metal, so it's stronger than a drilled hole. Corresponding holes in the blade were then aligned and red-hot slugs of metal were slotted in place through the holes. The ends of the slugs were then hammered flat to form rivets, securing the shaft to the blade. I was extremely proud to hammer my initials into the blade and claim it as my own! This was a shovel that looked like it would last for a thousand years. It could withstand a nuclear holocaust. It was a heavy old piece of kit. It was never going to blow over in a breeze and you definitely wouldn't want it round the back of the head!

THE NEXT STATION ON THIS JOURNEY WILL BE

Before I could use my shovel as a fireman, though, we needed somewhere for 5164 to go: a station. When the rail network was laid around the country, the stations, naturally, also slowly came into being. Some of these were great works of architecture where the architects really indulged themselves. There was no thought of making the main stations simple, workaday structures. The railway companies wanted to encourage people to use the railways, people who might actually be a bit frightened about travelling by train. It was said that if you were on a train travelling faster than the galloping speed of a horse – normally up to about 30mph – you wouldn't be able to breathe. You can sort of understand why the Victorians might have thought that. If you stick your head out of the window of a speeding car, facing into the wind, it is hard to catch a breath. You have to turn away from the direction of travel to suck in some calm air. Maybe they thought that travelling by train would be like that all the time. No one really knew, after all, what it was like to travel faster than a galloping horse.

Opposite: Most of the people who work so hard to keep the Severn Valley Railway running are volunteers.

To impress their fledgling passengers, and to give them a comforting feeling of reassurance, railway companies built their stations to look like stately homes or museums. These grand buildings suggested that travelling by train was to be looked forward to as much as a visit to a grand country house, or as safe as a trip to the library. Temple Meads station in Bristol was built in the style of a Tudor castle, while the station at Stoke-on-Trent looked more like a Jacobean stately home. Most impressive of all must be St Pancras in London, with the hotel that fronted the station looking like a Gothic palace.

Smaller stations out in the countryside took on the appearance of large cottages, or the gatehouses to local estates, and were run with unerring efficiency by the local stationmaster. Not only passengers, but all manner of freight would pass through the station; from foodstuffs and fancy goods to coal, gravel and the Royal Mail. Making sure that his station was always ready for passengers or freight was the stationmaster's job. He also supplemented his income by doing some private trading in goods passing through the station: if you needed a load of sand or wanted some fresh fish, he was the man to see.

The stationmaster was said to be as important to his local community as the doctor, the vicar or the local policeman, and was afforded the respect his status demanded. He generally lived in a house provided for him by the

Deep in discussion on the footplate of 5164.

railway company: he would either pay rent or the house would be taken into account in his salary which, at some stations close to London in the 1860s, could be as much as £230 a year. On top of that, the stationmaster could expect a bonus of up to 40 per cent of his salary if the company was doing well and he was running a tidy station. The stationmaster was responsible for making sure that the station was kept clean, that the woodwork and ironwork were smartly painted and that the station gardens looked splendid and weed-free. The station porter was the one who would actually tend the garden and, in the absence of a general handyman, would probably attend to the other maintenance jobs as well. He wouldn't be able to take any shortcuts and do a shoddy job, either, because most stationmasters started out their careers as lowly porters: they therefore knew all the tricks of the trade.

The stationmaster would probably have to move several times during his career, with his earnings increasing as he took over larger stations and had more staff to manage. Winning a 'Best Kept Station' award was a major achievement for an ambitious stationmaster. His ultimate aim would be to snare the top job at Paddington Station, where he would have to wear a top hat and frock coat to work and meet members of the Royal Family passing through on a regular basis.

I had a spell doing a spot of painting and weeding on the Severn Valley line and I have to admit that I preferred working on the engine. Keeping

5164 making steam
in the sunshine.

everything spick and span – including your own appearance – isn't really my strong point, but it was a huge part of the stationmaster's job. He was the public face of the railway and the railway companies were real public relations pioneers, persuading the whole country that taking the train was the only way to travel. The companies commissioned well-known artists to produce posters advertising holiday trips, something that was to become a huge part of the railway business.

MAKING A POINT

Another key player on any stretch of railway line was the signalman. These unsung heroes had one of the loneliest jobs; stuck out in a signal box for a twelve-hour shift, yet having to stay constantly alert. Their job, after all, was to pull levers to let engine drivers know whether it was safe to proceed. The levers were mounted on a lever frame inside the signal box (in the early days the signalman would have to trot between levers at different points on his stretch of track) and either changed the signal arms on signal towers at the side of the track, or operated points. Points were, and still are, moveable lengths of rail that can swing in and out of position on the track to guide the train into a siding or onto a different stretch of track. The signalman, whose job was deemed so important to the safe running of the railway that he had to sit a qualifying exam, be nominated by three company directors and appointed by two Justices of the Peace, was regularly required to work a seventy-two-hour week in his freezing signal box. Like other railway employees, he could be fined or sacked for the slightest misdemeanour and worked whatever shifts he was told to – all for the princely sum in the 1860s of about £1 per week.

Despite the fact that as early as the 1860s, well-respected doctors were publicly testifying that overworking staff like signalmen would inevitably lead to them making mistakes through fatigue (sometimes with tragic consequences), it wasn't until the industrial reforms of the early twentieth century that such key personnel were able to work sensible hours.

CHANGING TIMES

Sensible hours takes us on to yet another way that the railways changed the lives of people in Britain – railway time. Before the railways, accurate timekeeping didn't really matter that much. Within your own town or village, you would go by the church clock or the town hall clock and if you arranged to meet someone at 12.00 p.m., that would be 12.00 p.m. by the church clock – local time. Because nobody really travelled very far from their home towns, nobody cared that it was midday in London but in Bristol it was only twelve minutes to twelve. There was no TV, no radio, no telephone and, until it started being introduced on God's Wonderful Railway in 1839, no telegraph system.

Opposite: Contemplating my first shift as an engine driver with a trainload of passengers aboard.

The arrival of the railways changed all that. It wasn't only that if you didn't know the time you would miss your train. Best case scenario, you would miss your train – worst case scenario, your train would have a head-on collision. In order to have trains running between cities safely, to a rigid timetable, on a sensible schedule, everybody had to agree what time it was. This sounds totally sensible, but it was revolutionary thinking back in the nineteenth century. Remember that there are huge differences in Britain at different times of year between when the sun rises and sets in the north and in the south. For years, people had lived their lives by the rising and setting of the sun and many objected to the railway companies deciding what the time should be. GWR eventually decided in 1840 that, when it was 12 p.m. at Greenwich (GMT) it was 12 p.m. everywhere. It took years for all the other railway companies to accept the idea, but it did become known as 'Railway Time'. It wasn't until 1880 that the government put its foot down and said, 'Look, none of this mucking about, when it's 12 p.m. in London it's 12 p.m. everywhere.' Then everyone in Britain had to keep the same time. Yet Britain was the first country in the world to decide to adopt one standard time.

By 1880, the telegraph system had spread along the railway lines and that linked everywhere with London and GMT. Engine drivers, however, needed to know whether or not they were running on time and there was no way they could have a telegraph machine on the footplate. Instead, they carried the most accurate pocket watches of their era. I went to take a look at one in a workshop where antique watches are repaired and restored and was allowed to help adjust it. It was running fast, so it needed to have tiny weights screwed onto a flywheel cog that was part of the mechanism to slow it down.

I've got hundreds of screwdrivers and tools for my work but I don't have anything that would have fitted the delicate little screw heads I had to work on. I had to use watchmakers' micro tools and for someone who's used to working on trucks and had just been working on massive great steam engines, I suddenly felt like the clumsiest creature on the planet. I was like a giant trying to pick up single grains of sand with his fingers, except I couldn't actually use my fingers: not just because of the grease and oil that's usually caked on them, but because the cogs and gears in the watch were so delicate that the sweat from your hands could corrode them. You have to use tweezers and special tools to dismantle an antique watch, and I was warned that with something as old as this it only takes a second to destroy it. As if I wasn't nervous enough already! I could hardly stop my hands shaking.

I had to strip the watch down so that extra washers could be added to the balance mechanism. These were tiny, tiny washers the size of a pinhead, kept in a test tube like some kind of alien insect. You have to pick them up with a special screwdriver attachment: it was all so intricate and I was concentrating so hard that I had to remind myself to breathe. The two little washers seemed to weigh nothing to me, but they made sure that the watch

Above opposite: A little bit of Brasso gave the numbers a proud shine.

Below opposite: The engine driver's pocket watch was an essential and delicate piece of kit.

Having a fully working whistle on a locomotive was a legal requirement.

was running sweetly and the only thing that I really did wrong was having oily truck mechanic fingers that left marks on the dial. These were cleaned off by rolling a piece of Blu-Tack® across it, so all was well in the end. It's amazing how careful a Victorian engine driver must have been with such a timepiece, especially when his whole world was full of grease and oil and soot and coal dust.

WHISTLING FOR IT!

Now that I had a shovel and a watch (actually, I used my own rather than risk an antique) I was finally ready to serve on the footplate of 5164. The old girl herself, though, still needed one last touch before she could leave Bridgnorth: a whistle. It is illegal for an engine to set out along a railway without some kind of whistle, horn or other highly audible, unmistakable warning device.

5164 shows off her brand new whistle.

The steam whistle, so the story goes, was first introduced in 1833 after an accident on a level crossing between Bagworth and Thornton in Leicestershire. Engine driver Martin Weatherburn smashed his engine, *Samson*, into a cart carrying hundreds of eggs and fifty pounds of butter: it made quite an omelette! Weatherburn himself was in serious trouble over the incident, despite the fact that no one was hurt. In those early days, the railway owners took a very dim view of anything that brought bad publicity and might affect business. It was all very well for navvies to die while the railways were being built, but accidents on a railway that was open to passenger and freight traffic would discourage people from using the service – and that meant less profit.

Weatherburn claimed that he had sounded his horn – he would have blown a horn like the ones they used for fox hunting – but either the cart driver hadn't heard him or just ignored it. Actually, the cart driver might have thought he had plenty of time as he probably didn't have a clue about steam engines or how fast they could move. As it happened, Weatherburn's father was good friends with George Stephenson, who discussed the matter with the railway company's directors. They all agreed that a better warning sound was needed, preferably steam powered to make it really loud.

Stephenson visited a musical instrument maker in Leicester. He worked with him to produce a steam trumpet that was demonstrated to the company directors just ten days later. The steam trumpet was about eighteen inches long with a mouth about six inches wide and worked well enough for the directors to approve it for installation on all of their locomotives. The idea quickly caught on: different types of whistle were developed and it soon became compulsory to sound them under certain circumstances, such as approaching a level crossing.

The whistle for 5164 was made from scratch from plans for a GWR whistle dated 1930, so it was pretty much spot on in terms of being from the right period. It was different from Stephenson's steam trumpet in that pulling a lever opened a valve that let steam into a brass cup, from where it escaped via a thin opening up into an elongated bell. The steam alternately compressed or rarefied in the bell, all of which produced the vibration and resonance that created the sound.

The final part to be made was a nut that screwed onto the top of the whistle and held it all together. Even making this one small component needed a horrendous amount of preparation to set up the milling machine for total accuracy. Working out the exact cutting speed required took a lot of maths: that was never my strong point but I had a Bridgnorth engineer called Tom to help me. A few sums and several cups of tea later, our nut came out perfectly and polished up a treat. It was just the job for the top of the whistle.

> The shovel that I made was a good deal bigger and heavier than the one usually used by a Severn Valley fireman, but it did a grand job.

A quick brew? Where better to keep your cuppa warm than on a shelf above the coal hole?

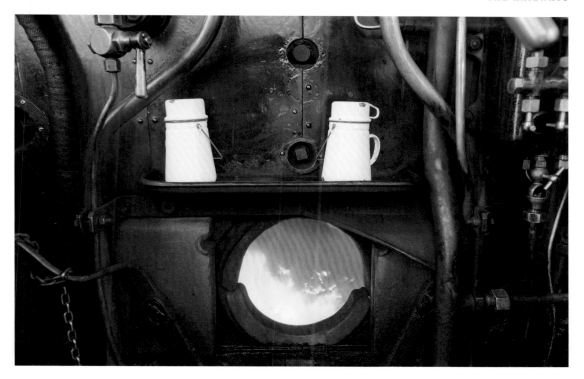

FULL STEAM AHEAD

Once we had fitted the whistle on top of 5164, we were finally ready to set off for the old girl's first day out in a long while. We had a passenger roster of specially invited guests, mainly friends and relatives of the Severn Valley Railway team, and I couldn't get over how excited they all were. From the oldest among them, who could remember when steam power ruled the railways, to the smallest kids, they were all bubbling over. You don't get that on the 8.45 to Waterloo! People love steam trains. I think it's because they seem almost alive, like great, big fiery monsters – friendly monsters, though. If the passengers were all excited, and they were only riding in the lovely old carriages, I was on cloud nine. Not only was I to have a go as a fireman but this was also to be my first train-driving lesson! When I climbed up onto the footplate, it all felt a bit familiar. I'd been up there before, when I climbed inside the firebox, but this seemed familiar in the way that climbing into the cab of a truck is familiar. We were about to take this massive machine for a spin, after all. It's only when you reach the locomotive's cab that you immediately see there is no steering wheel. Suddenly it's not quite so familiar after all . . .

The thing that really strikes you when you're on the footplate of a steam locomotive, all fired up and ready to go, is the smell. It's a lovely mixture of warm oil and grease and the smell of a roaring coal fire. My first job was to feed the fire, using my wrought-iron shovel. It's hot work shovelling coal into a furnace like that, especially when you're using a shovel made from solid wrought iron. Looking back, we might have done well to put a wooden handle on the thing, because you really felt the weight of it when the blade was piled with coal. While I was shovelling, enjoying the hard graft and nattering away, wired for sound with everything I said going straight back to the director's earphones, I said something like: 'By heck, much more of this and I'll have muscles on me . . .'
'GUY!!!'

When it came to driving 5164, I was feeling a bit nervous. The old girl had only just gone back on the rails and I didn't want to do her any damage. On the other hand, I wasn't up there all by myself and the Severn Valley guys weren't about to let me wreck their pride and joy! Apart from anything else, there were too many gauges and dials for me to take in all at once. Any steam loco in passenger service had controls that operated everything from the cylinder drain cocks (these allow any water from condensed steam sitting in the cylinders to be blown out in a cloud of steam as the locomotive starts to move) to the steam-heating pressure valve, which fed steam to heating pipes in the train carriages.

The controls that I needed to concentrate on were as follows: the brake valve (you have to apply the brakes really gently to avoid locking the wheels); the regulator, which controls the flow of steam to the cylinders and is, basically, the accelerator; and the screw reverser. You have to be as gentle with the regulator as you do with the brake valve for completely the opposite reason: too much steam too fast will have the wheels spinning. The screw reverser, meanwhile, controls how far the pistons travel and which side of the piston is supplied with steam. If you have that turned the wrong way you could easily set off backwards instead of forwards!

> Preparing a traditional firebox fry-up on my hot shovel.

I don't think that I did too badly on my first outing as an engine driver. I did briefly spin the wheels slightly once, but I don't think anyone noticed. Well, no one except the Severn Valley lads, the film crew and most of the passengers! All in all, we had a fantastic day for our run along the Severn Valley Railway, riding in a beautifully restored tribute to Britain's past industrial achievement, calling at lovingly maintained, nostalgic stations and steaming through gorgeous countryside in glorious sunshine. I even managed to heat up my shovel in the firebox to fry up a traditional, engine driver's bacon-and-egg sandwich on the hot blade. That's what I call a heck of a day out.

A bacon-and-egg
sandwich never
tasted so good.

FROM **FARM** TO **FACTORY**

If you had been born in 1801, you would most likely have been born not in a hospital but at home and your home would almost certainly have been in the countryside: at that time, only around 20 per cent of Britain's population lived in towns. That, though, was all about to change. Within fifty years, more than 50 per cent of us would be 'townies'. During this era, places like Glasgow and Bradford grew to become home to more than eight times as many people. Manchester mushroomed from a town of 88,000 in 1801 (a small town by today's standards) to more than 642,000 in 1901 (a pretty big town by anybody's standards). In London, the population was already over a million people by 1801 and that figure rose to more than three million by 1861. That's a fair few people, yet it's only a threefold increase. So why were the northern towns growing so much faster?

The answer is the machine age, spawning new industries that were drawing workers into the towns from the countryside just as the machines were also depriving those in the countryside of work. Britain's great Industrial Revolution was sweeping the people off the land and into the factories, and these factories were predominantly in the north.

Before the factories were built, there was no such thing as mass production. Instead there were 'cottage industries', where people would be making things at home or in a workshop. The village blacksmith, for example, would make and repair all sorts of things from horseshoes, spades and nails to plough blades, hooks, hammers and swords. A local weaver would have a handloom set up in his own house, producing cloth from wool that would be produced nearby, and spun into yarn even closer to home – perhaps by his wife. Before the factories the majority of people in Britain weren't involved in manufacturing, they were primarily employed in agriculture ... working on the land.

Throughout the course of the eighteenth century, farmworkers had seen different machines make their jobs redundant. It was when the threshing machine came along in 1784, however, that they really started to feel they were being squeezed out. Threshing – the process of separating harvested grain from the stalks and husks – had always been labour intensive. It was hard graft, but proper work for farm labourers. The threshing machine, though, could do the whole job more quickly and more efficiently than even the most experienced gang of farm workers. When portable steam engines (and later self-propelled traction engines) came along to power the

Right: Factories in Sheffield belching out smoke in the nineteenth century.

Opposite:
A threshing machine in use around 1900.

Four of the Tolpuddle Martyrs who all emigrated to Canada after their release.
Left to right:
James Brine, Thomas Standfield, John Standfield and James Loveless.

threshing machines, it was the beginning of the end for mass employment in the countryside.

Even before the arrival of the threshing machine, farm workers had been feeling the pinch as many of them had been accustomed to being able to keep a few animals themselves, to make ends meet. They grazed sheep or cows, kept geese or even grew their own food on common land, but between 1770 and 1830, more than six million acres of common land was taken from the ordinary people, snatched by rich landowners, who had been given the right to do so by Acts of Parliament – the Inclosure Acts. By enclosing common land, the lords of the manor and their wealthy tenant farmers gave the local populace no option but to work for them – and that gave the rich landowners even more control over working conditions and wages. The poor were getting poorer as the rich were getting richer.

In 1830, the desperate situation of the farm workers led to the Swing Riots. Beginning in Kent in August, 1830, the riots had spread across the whole of southern England by the end of the year. The farm workers did not attack the landowners and burn their mansions, as you might expect, but instead directed their anger at the machines. In Kent alone, over a hundred threshing machines were destroyed. Threatening letters, often signed with the fictitious name 'Captain Swing', were sent to local farm owners and magistrates, demanding better wages. The tactics worked to a degree, but at a huge cost to the protesters: 2,000 were arrested, almost 650 were sent to prison, nearly 500 were sent to penal colonies in Australia, and nineteen sent to the gallows. Four years later, a group of farm workers in Dorset were arrested for forming a Friendly Society – basically a trade union – and refusing to work for less than ten shillings a week.

The Tolpuddle Martyrs, as they became known, weren't arrested for threatening anyone or for wrecking machinery; they were charged because a landowner discovered an old law that made it illegal for ordinary people to swear an oath to each other, and the union men had sworn to remain true to one another and their cause. Half a dozen men were transported to Australia to face hard labour, and though the men's families and supporters collected 800,000 signatures calling for their release, it took two years for them to be set free.

It's no accident that these incidents took place in the south of the country, where farmers faced very little in the way of competition in the labour market. Up north, those who could no longer make a living working on the land were better able to find work elsewhere – in the new factories. Just as the spread of steam power was unstoppable, so the great exodus from the countryside to the cities was well underway.

I PLOUGH THE FIELDS (AND THEY SCATTER...)

By the 1860s, fields that had previously been ploughed using a team of horses to pull a single blade through the soil were being turned over using steam power and a whole new set of skills were being introduced to agriculture. It was a man called John Fowler who developed the idea of using steam engines for ploughing, winning a £500 prize in 1858 for the system that he came up with. Fowler's idea used a steam engine parked at one end of the field and a pulley system anchored at the other end, with a cable running between the two. The cable was wound by the steam engine and attached to the cable was the plough, which was dragged through the soil.

I had a go on a similar set-up with a great big steam traction engine at either end of a field. As the ploughman, I had to sit on the plough and guide it along, steering it with a wheel that was almost comically huge. Because there's no power steering or suchlike that you might find on a modern vehicle, you need a steering wheel that big to keep the plough on course. You can't do it just by twiddling a little knob. I doubt that steering wheel would even fit inside my Astra van. I might have struggled to keep my furrows straight, but for a Victorian ploughman used to walking behind a plough pulled by heavy horses, fighting to guide the blade as it bucked and baulked through every heavy patch of soil, steering a steam-drawn plough must have seemed like luxury.

Turning the plough around at the edge of the field was proper hard work. It's a heavy old piece of kit with blades and steering gear at either end, carefully balanced so that only the rear end where the driver and his mate sit is in contact with the soil. Lifting the blades out of the ground to line the plough up for the next run needed two of us hanging from the 'front' set to tip the balance, lift the rear blades out of the ground and turn what had been the front into the back. It took a lot of effort, but once the plough was hooked up to the drag lines again, it was soon trundling along at a cracking pace.

Steam-powered ploughing in this way could turn over a field twenty times faster than a man walking behind a Shire horse and did it with four blades cutting the soil instead of just one. That, of course, was the sort of mechanisation that put a lot of people out of work. But mechanisation was creating work, too, and of a more regular variety. Machines like the steam engines and the plough were built in factories, and these factories offered a steady wage with year-round work: agricultural work, by contrast, was often seasonal.

MILLS AND BOOM

Not all factories were crammed into the hearts of the burgeoning new cities. Some were in far more remote locations, such as Gayle Mill in North Yorkshire, which we visited a couple of times while filming the TV series. Gayle Mill was built in 1784 by entrepreneurs Oswald and Thomas Routh, who saw the expanding cotton industry as a sound investment. The end of the war in America, which had won its independence from Britain, meant that the transatlantic 'triangular trade' route was flourishing once more. Triangular trade involved manufactured goods such as cloth, guns, tools

> Steam engines and ploughs like these turned over a field twenty times faster than their horse-drawn equivalents.

This old tea pot is a vital piece of kit at Gayle Mill.

and other metal goods being exported from British ports to the west coast of Africa. Slaves were then carried as cargo from Africa across the Atlantic to the Caribbean and America; finally, cotton and tobacco were shipped back across the Atlantic to Britain. The three legs of the trade route formed the Atlantic triangle, the most controversial part of the system being the slaves kidnapped in Africa to be sold in America. It seems almost unbelievable to us now, doesn't it? But for many years the slave trade made a lot of people in Britain a lot of money.

The cotton arrived at Liverpool docks, which had grown since the first part of the commercial docks was established in 1715 to become Britain's second busiest port, after London. The importance of Liverpool, and later Manchester after the opening of the ship canal in 1894, to the cotton business was that they were in the north of the country, which was the best place for weaving. Down south, the air was too dry and cotton yarn was liable to dry out and snap, which caused delays in production while the problem was sorted. In the north, the damp atmosphere meant that breaking yarns was less of a problem. Raw cotton, however, is a bulky commodity, difficult and expensive to transport, so shipping it direct to the north west was the obvious thing to do.

Plenty of moisture and rain meant that there were also plenty of streams to turn the water wheels that powered most of the cotton mills, at least

The tea pot has been used as an oil can for as long as anyone can remember!

Oiling the bearings on the main drive shaft at Gayle Mill.

before steam engines came along. So, even though it isn't in the middle of an industrial town, Gayle Mill wasn't too badly situated. It had a ready supply of water from Gayle Beck to turn its mill wheel and the locals had long been involved in knitting as a cottage industry. They worked on the land, but also hand-knitted garments using locally produced wool: some of them would even knit as they walked to work in the fields! The Rouths knew that they had a local workforce that was familiar with textiles and they reckoned that a new road that had been built from the west was the answer to any potential transport problems.

They were right, for a time. When the mill first opened there were only twenty like it in the whole country. Seventy years later there were nearly 2,000 and Manchester was where it was all happening – the people called the city 'Cottonopolis'. In 1789, an advertisement was placed in the *Manchester Mercury* offering Gayle Mill for sale. Bringing cotton in and shipping finished yarn out was clearly proving to be a more expensive transport problem than the Rouths had anticipated. They failed to find a buyer for their business, and the mill soldiered on.

Gayle Mill was a very practical design for the time; a thoroughly modern factory in a rural setting. It was arranged over three floors, with internal hoists to lift loads through trapdoors between floors. The raw cotton bales were delivered to the top floor where the cotton was beaten or 'scrutched', to clean out all the dust and seeds. All done by hand, this was dirty, exhausting work, yet was work deemed suitable for women and children.

The cleaned cotton was dropped through a trapdoor to the middle floor where the cotton fibres, already separated a bit by the scrutching, were straightened and untangled by carding. Initially, this would also have been done by hand, using carding combs, but there were eventually carding and roving machines that stretched the cotton into a kind of yarn. The yarn, which had no real strength as the fibres were still quite loose, was then passed to the lower floor where the spinning machines turned it into thread. This was wound onto bobbins and despatched in consignments to the weaving works in Lancashire.

It wasn't a production line in the way that Henry Ford would have it when he began building cars in Detroit, but for the time, this was pretty much state of the art. The system at Gayle Mill had been pioneered by a businessman called Richard Arkwright, who set up a water-powered mill at Cromford in Derbyshire in 1771. Arkwright subsequently established other mills out in the countryside where he had a good water supply for power. He overcame the problem of not having enough local workers in rural areas by bringing them in from elsewhere, building homes for them and creating what became known as 'factory villages'.

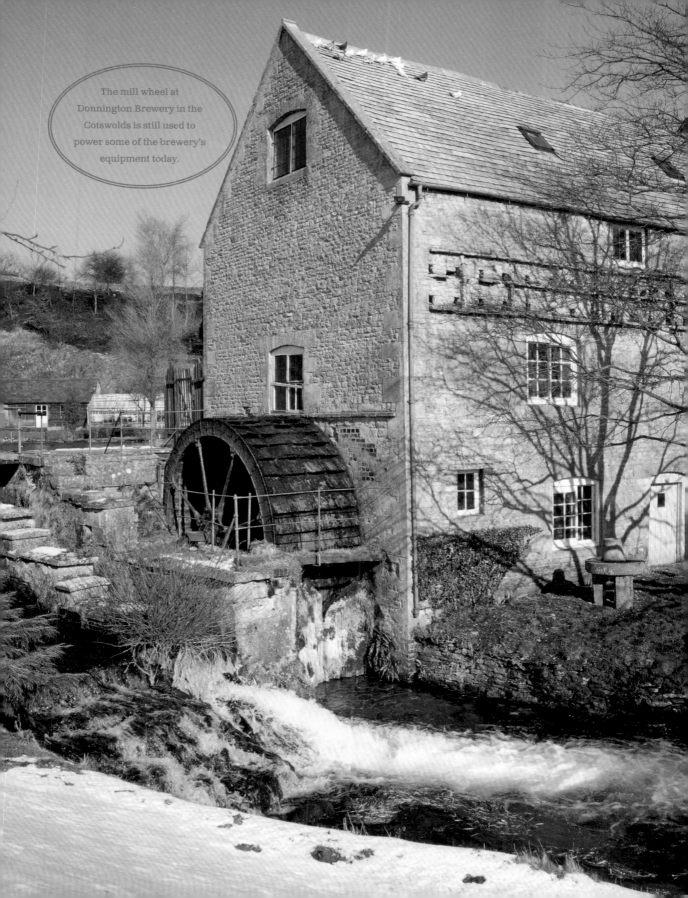

The mill wheel at Donnington Brewery in the Cotswolds is still used to power some of the brewery's equipment today.

But the country mills found it difficult to compete with city factories, where steam power was proving to be far more reliable and transport was not a problem. Gayle Mill was a good example of an enterprise where the supply and transport problems made it difficult to compete. When the mill was squeezed out of the cotton business, it went over to spinning first locally produced flax – flax being the plant that is used to produce linen – and then wool for the local knitting cottage industry (specifically to be used in making socks). The woollen mill prospered for a while but when it fell on hard times again it was partially decommissioned: the building was turned into residential accommodation for a few years during the nineteenth century.

Then, in 1879, Gayle Mill went back to work as a factory. The latest industrial woodworking lathes, saws, drills and planes were installed and it became a sawmill. When the railway had come to nearby Hawes a few years earlier in 1876, it had revitalised the whole area: there was now plenty of work manufacturing parts for carts, fence posts, roof beams and all manner of wooden produce. The factory tended to run on a seasonal basis: the winter months were spent acquiring and stockpiling raw materials, with trees felled locally and stored as timber to dry or 'season' in preparation for use in the mill; spring and summer were the manufacturing months before the process returned to tree felling in the autumn.

A romanticised winter image of an exhausted mother and daughter after a shift at a mill.

DARK SATANIC MILLS

When the factory was operating, whether as a cotton mill or a sawmill, it worked just like a factory in a big town or city. A bell was rung to call the workers into the mill first thing in the morning, there was another bell for dinner (lunch is dinner up north, remember) and a final bell at home time. Village and family life revolved around the bell: sounds like being back at school, doesn't it? For those working in factories in the cities, however, factory life was far stricter than in any school.

Like the rural factory owners, industrialists in the cities realised that they needed their workforce close at hand. They built streets of terraced houses,

Few factories bore
any resemblance
to this Victorian
illustration of a
spacious, clean,
well-lit mill.

typically with two rooms downstairs and two rooms upstairs. In the early days, these houses had no running water, with a whole street having to share an outdoor pump. Outside toilets were also shared by a number of houses and rubbish was dumped in a sewer running down the middle of the street. Factory workers packed themselves into these houses, with several families sharing the four rooms and splitting the rent owed to the mill owners. Slum conditions like these are, of course, a perfect breeding ground for disease and there were regular outbreaks of cholera and typhus. It didn't take long for the bosses to realise that a workforce that was dying off from preventable diseases was not good for business. Consequently, the workers' housing was slowly improved.

While living conditions for factory workers did get better, the environments in which they lived and worked were still far from ideal. Entire families worked in the mills and a twelve-hour factory shift from 6.00 a.m. to 6.00 p.m. was regarded as a normal day. Sixteen-hour stints were not uncommon: that wasn't overtime, either, but a standard shift. The factory bell or hooter might sound as early as 5.00 a.m. and if you weren't inside the factory doors ready to start work an hour later, you were locked out. There were no excuses for arriving late when the gaffer knew that you only lived ten minutes' walk away. You lost a day's wages and, more than likely, the next day's wages as well, as a fine for not showing up.

A young lad working barefoot in a Mancheser cotton mill in 1909.

The long hours meant that, for much of the year, workers were going to work before dawn and coming back after sunset. Even when they did see daylight, the smoke from the factories' steam engines (by 1850, 86 per cent of all factories relied on steam power) and the furnaces of the engineering works, combined with smoke from the coal fires or stoves that were the only source of heat in every home, created an almost permanent dark cloud over the area. Dark satanic mills? When William Blake coined the phrase in the poem that we know as 'Jerusalem', he didn't know the half of it. The quality of the air that people were breathing on the way to work was very poor, but when they got into the factory, it was even worse. In the engineering works, there would be all sorts of smoke and dust drifting in the atmosphere; in the mills it was cotton fibres and dust that people had to contend with. It didn't help that water was often sprayed on the floor to keep the dust down, or that steam pipes were set up to spray steam into the air high above the heads of the workers to keep the atmosphere damp. This meant that workers were breathing in moist air and their clothes were never really dry.

Lung disease and stomach disorders became an occupational hazard for factory workers. Seldom seeing sunshine led to a lack of vitamin D and this, along with a poor diet, meant that children's bones didn't grow properly. Kids from the factory communities were less likely to grow tall and strong, and far more likely to have the bowed or 'bandy' legs associated with rickets.

It was to protect these children in particular that the government introduced legislation in the form of the Factory Acts. In 1833, a third of the workers in textile factories were children or boys between the ages of eight and seventeen. The factory owners liked employing children because they could pay them less than adults. The bosses had no problem with childish bad behaviour: the child's parents (unless the kid had been hired from an orphanage or workhouse) were most likely also working in the factory and would be disciplined if their son or daughter misbehaved. Not only were they cheap labour, but children were also small enough to squeeze underneath machinery to tie up loose threads, or to clean out muck and waste that was threatening to clog up the works. Because they could crawl in to do this, there was no need to switch off the machines to carry out these tasks, and hence there was no loss in production. This was often dangerous work but, as one manager told a factory inspector in 1864, 'They seldom lose a hand … it only takes off a finger.'

The Factory Act of 1802 forced factory owners to provide proper ventilation and to supply children working for them with two complete outfits of clothing. Children between the ages of nine and thirteen could work only eight hours a day and those between fourteen and eighteen a maximum of twelve hours. Children under nine were officially banned from working and had to go to school instead. Not only that, but the factory owners were made responsible for building the new schools for their workers' children.

Young workers
in a mill in
Manchester.

By 1819, children under sixteen years were limited by law to a seventy-two-hour working week and a further Factory Act in 1833 decreed that children up to thirteen years old could not work more than eight hours a day without a lunch break. The children were also required to have a minimum of two hours of formal education each day. In 1848, the 'Ten Hours Act' limited all workers to a ten-hour day. Industry responded by making nighttime working commonplace and keeping the factories running constantly with ten-hour shifts day and night.

In the mid-1880s, a chap called Tom Mann started to make a bit of a name for himself as a champion of workers' rights. He published a pamphlet calling for a standard eight-hour working day, became involved in a number of different strikes and encouraged the trades unions to adopt the eight-hour day as one of their main goals. His demands would be a long time coming: most workers didn't enjoy a standard eight-hour working day until well into the next century.

While at Gayle Mill, we watched some film from the early 1900s that showed weavers working in a factory. It really helped to make sense of everything that we had been learning about factory life. The machines were packed

Gayle Mill was built alongside the tumbling waters of Gayle Beck, using the river to drive its water wheel, now long gone.

in pretty tight and there were no real safety guards to protect the people working on them. It was clear that the factory wasn't there for the workers, but was all about the mill owners and making money. One kid in the film looked as if he wasn't more than twelve years old.

Watching the women on the film leaving the factory, it struck me that they all looked happy and were smiling. That may have been because there were some strange men there filming them – not something that would have happened every day – but they certainly seemed to have a spring in their step. These women really were 'happy campers' and, for people who were worked hard for long hours and paid a pittance, none of them looked like skinny slaves being worked to death, and I certainly didn't spot anyone suffering from the 'obesity epidemic' that plagues Britain in the twenty-first century. They all looked reasonably fit.

For those who had jobs, money to keep a roof over their heads and put food on the table, maybe these glory days of British industrial might weren't always as bad for the poor downtrodden workers as we are often led to believe, although no one could deny that vast improvements to working conditions for those who laboured in Britain's factories were sorely needed. Yet Britain was known then as 'the workshop of the world'. Can we still say that now? I don't think we can.

WATER, WATER EVERYWHERE

We weren't at Gayle Mill just to watch old documentaries. There is, you see, a unique feature about the place. Far from those dark satanic mills in the cities, out in the beautiful Wensleydale countryside, Gayle let the steam age pass right on by and stuck with water power. The big water wheel, however, was done away with, and a special kind of turbine was installed instead. The idea of using water turbines was not exactly new – the Romans were using them as long ago as the fourth century – but the great advances in metallurgy and engineering in the nineteenth century meant that turbines were now far more efficient and boasted impressive power output.

Designed by Professor James Thomson of Queen's College, Belfast, Gayle's innovative double vortex turbine was installed in 1879. The turbine was built by an engineering firm in Kendal called Williamson Brothers and was a very clever piece of machinery. It was a sealed unit, with the two parts of the casing, like two five-foot-high dustbin lids, bolted together all around the outside. Water was fed into the casing from a supply pipe, and it rushed around the outside of the turbine before it was fed through specially positioned vanes that directed it in a spiral towards the centre where the water vortex – like a whirlpool – turned a shaft. The same thing was happening inside both halves of the casing, which is why the turbine was known as a 'double vortex'.

Opposite: The weirs were built to help control the flow of water down to where the twenty-foot-high water wheel turned at the side of the building by the riverbank.

Although it was using the same water supply as the original huge water wheel, the turbine produced twice the power despite being a fraction of its size. The shaft supplied the equivalent of eleven horsepower: belts transferred this power from the spinning shaft up into the factory, where another shaft ran the length of the building. From that shaft, a series of belts and pulleys powered the woodworking lathes, the planing bench and the saw. There was enough power to run all of the factory machines at once.

Unfortunately, the turbine was out of action when we went to see it because it had sprung a leak and had to be shut down. This wasn't just a few drips, mind you, it was losing forty-three litres of water a second – that's a fair old amount of water. For those of you concerned about the environment, don't worry. The water was all leaking back into Gayle Beck and flowing on down the valley.

Examining the twin vortex turbine at Gayle Mill.

Having mentioned the environment, though, it does make you think back to the city factories with their smoke and soot. Here at Gayle there would have been none of that. There would have been smoke – mainly wood smoke – from the fires or stoves in local houses, but no factory chimney belching out into the atmosphere. The employees at Gayle would have walked to work in the fresh air of the Dales, not spluttering through the smog of the city. I know where I would rather have been.

Tony first came to work at Gayle Mill as an apprentice in the 1960s and is now very much involved with Gayle Mill Trust and the restoration of the building. We joined him to help fix the leak. In order to sort that out, we had to find out what was causing it, and that meant splitting open the two dishes that formed the main casing. We had to take out all of the bolts around the lip of the 'clam shell' and Tony warned me that if I dropped one down into the sluice – where the waste water drained off back into the river – I'd be the one going to get it, because down there it was dirty, wet and very cold! There was snow blowing through on the hills outside and inside the mill was very cold – just as it would have been when it was a working factory. We were lucky, if that is the word, to be experiencing the same conditions as the nineteenth-century workers had done.

Although only a fraction of the size, the turbine could produce twice the power of the water wheel it replaced.

Tony told me that no one so much as laid a spanner on the turbine from the time it was installed until something finally went wrong in the 1970s. Even then, all that had happened was that a bolt had sheared, not in the turbine itself, but on one of the control arms. It didn't need an expensive repair: as Tony put it, 'the bits cost ten bob,' and then had to explain to me that 'ten bob' was 50p in new money. Come on, Tony, we've had decimal currency since 1971, so it must have been 50p then as well! The point is, after a century in operation, the only repair this turbine needed cost just 50p. That sort of reliability doesn't come built in with many of today's machines, does it?

Will, the mill boss, came down to help use wedges and crowbars to prize the two halves of the turbine apart. It had to be done slowly and carefully, inch by inch, to make sure that we didn't buckle, bend or break anything – including ourselves. It was then that I dropped one of the wedges down into the sluice. Tony just sighed, shook his head and told me to go and get it. He's not the sort of bloke who's wrong about anything very often and he was definitely right about it being dirty, wet and very cold when I climbed down into that sluice!

Once we had opened up the turbine casing enough to see what was going on inside, it was clear that while the turbine was still spinning freely and working perfectly, the plates that directed water into the mechanism had worked themselves loose. I was mightily impressed that we were the first people to see the inside of the turbine since it had been installed – the first men to work on it for more than a century. Gayle Mill is reckoned to be the oldest working turbine still installed in its original situation and doing its original job in Europe – possibly even in the world.

Clearly, it wasn't going to take a great deal to put the turbine right. We needed to replace a few parts, but I was really keen to get it working again as quickly as possible so that we could try it out and bring in some timber to work on upstairs. Not that I wanted to waste good timber; I didn't want to cut it up just for the sake of it. We needed to think of something useful that we could make using the machines powered by the double vortex turbine.

TIMBER!

In the meantime, if we were going to do some woodworking at the mill, we needed some wood. To get this, we needed to cut down a tree. Naturally, we had to do it just the way it would have been done in the nineteenth century. Or, to be perfectly honest, the way it might have been done.

Most of the wood they use at the mill when producing garden gates, fence posts and the like is sourced locally. We chose an old elm tree to cut down that was just a couple of miles away. Back then, clearing trees from farmland was a major undertaking when all you could use were axes, spades, horses and hard graft. I had some extra help in the shape of my mate Mave who's a joiner, not a lumberjack, but he knows his trees (if you're wondering why

Opposite: Smoky city streets or country lanes? I know where I'd rather walk to work.

he's called Mave, it's a nickname that comes from his real name, Mark Davis), and an 1875 traction engine called *The Chief*.

We used a two-man saw, just as they would have done in the Victorian age – no chainsaw cheating for us – and Mave explained how you have to pull, not push, to keep the blade under tension for a straight cut. The tree was dead, but even so, it was still hard going. While I was working up a sweat, Mave – who had clearly been doing his homework – told me that the world record for cutting down a twenty-inch diameter tree is 4.77 seconds. It took us a good while longer than that just to get our cut biting into the tree trunk! We were at it for the thick end of an hour and had still only got halfway through. I don't think that we were in line to break any world records.

At this point, I reckoned that the traction engine, which we had intended to use to take our timber to the mill, might be able to pull on the tree and provide a bit of tension to open up the cut. Knowing what a job the steam-powered winch did on dragging my plough across that field, I was sure that once I got my hands on the controls of the traction engine, we could cut out some of the hard work. The engine driver confirmed that steam power was our way forward and, with a rope attached to the tree, we applied a little tension. The tree, well dead and sitting in soft soil on the bank of a stream, leaned over a bit and then, with a little more encouragement from me at the controls of the traction engine, popped out of the ground like a cork from a bottle.

Once we had trimmed the tree trunk, it was loaded onto a trailer behind the traction engine. Mave and I then had the awesome task of driving the twenty-ton engine back to the mill. Driving *The Chief* is very much a two-man job. One of you has to steer – and that's not easy because you have to turn the steering wheel right to go left and left to go right. The other person controls the power: you've got gears and a throttle, but there are no brakes or pedals like you have on a truck. To speed up and slow down, you have to use your own judgement.

Mave had never been this close to a traction engine before, let alone driven one, but I was well up for it. We had a bit of a practice on the farmland and we must have been doing okay because *The Chief's* owners were happy for us to take it out on the road. I shovelled coal into the firebox while Mave nervously guided *The Chief* along the narrow Yorkshire country lanes at a stately 6mph. You might think that a bike racer used to taking roads like these at 160mph would be a bit bored with 6mph – but not a bit of it. There's a lot to do to keep *The Chief* on the move: stoking the boiler, keeping an eye on the pressure, making sure you're in the right gear, and checking that Mave hasn't had a nervous breakdown behind the steering wheel. On top of which, it's a real honour to drive an engine like this. It's part of our industrial heritage, part of our history, and there aren't many like it still in working

Opposite: Mave and me doing our best to guide *The Chief* back to Gayle Mill.

The restored Victorian hand-cranked crane that we used to deliver our timber to the mill.

order. To be honest, you really wouldn't want to go much faster than 6mph in a twenty-ton beast with no brakes. *The Chief* would take some stopping.

Driving *The Chief* would have been a real job. It's not like getting up, jumping into your van, turning the key and away you go. *The Chief*'s crew would have to be up at five in the morning to light the fire in the firebox and slowly heat the boiler. You don't want all that metal getting too hot too fast; metal might warp or rivets could pop. The fire would be built up slowly until the engine got up steam. You'd then set off for a day's graft: hauling lumber, ploughing fields, and taking on jobs for as long as there was daylight good enough for you to work in.

The Chief was originally dismantled and put into storage some time around 1920. It didn't see the light of day again until 2005. The restoration work took fully three years: the lads who restored the engine had to make a lot of parts from scratch and they have done a superb job. Given all their hard work, I felt fully justified in insisting that we drive it into a ford to wash off the mud we had managed to get splattered on the underside and clogged into the giant treads on the wheels. We had a bit of wheel spin and some slithering about on the stones in the ford, but Mave, even though he was still far from comfortable as helmsman, coped admirably. The thing that took real teamwork, though, was negotiating the narrow entrance to the lane leading into Gayle Mill. We had just a foot or so clearance on each side: one nudge from *The Chief* would have destroyed a neighbour's immaculate stone garden wall on one side, or the local telephone box on the other. With Mave adjusting his steering to get the right line and me dropping *The Chief* in and out of gear to control our speed, we inched our way forward … and breathed a huge sigh of relief when we made it without causing any damage.

Champion cyclist
James Moore *(right)*
won the world's first
bike race on a wooden
bicycle in 1868.

We used the mill's original (fully restored) Victorian crane, hand-cranked by Mave, to lift our timber off the flatbed trailer and lowered it down to where it would be sawn into workable timber. Actually, we had to cheat a bit here for the TV show. It takes months, even years, for a freshly felled tree to 'season' sufficiently to be used. Our tree wouldn't go to waste, though. It would replace the timber that we were going to use to produce – and Mave couldn't quite believe it when I told him – a bike.

PEDAL POWER

Now it's no secret that I'm pretty passionate about bikes. I race motorcycles and I also race the pedal variety – the motorcycles in road races and the pedal variety on mountain courses. You might think that to build a bicycle I would want a mechanic rather than a joiner like Mave, but you'd be wrong. The first proper pedal-powered bicycle was actually made of wood. And if you think that a wooden bike isn't something that could ever be raced, then think again. The first organised bicycle race was held in Paris in 1868 and was won by an Englishman, James Moore, riding a wooden bike with iron tyres.

The development of the simple bicycle closely followed the development of the Industrial Revolution, from the early part of the nineteenth century all the way into the fully industrialised twentieth century and beyond. A German inventor named Karl von Drais first took a trip on a bicycle of his own design in 1817, but it wasn't a bike as we know it. It had two wheels and a saddle but no pedals: instead, the rider sat astride the machine and 'walked' the thing along. Presumably, once you had got up enough speed or were rolling downhill, you would be able to lift your feet and cruise along. The first bicycle to use pedal power didn't appear until 1839, when Scottish blacksmith Kirkpatrick MacMillan devised the MacMillan velocipede. The pedals still weren't quite like the modern versions, however. Instead of turning a cog that spins the rear wheel via a chain, they operated crank arms, a bit like on a steam locomotive, that transferred the pedal power to the rear wheel. Like the German bike, the Scottish bike was made of wood, and it was MacMillan's design that we were going to replicate for my bike.

That meant taking a look at a MacMillan velocipede up close, which is a bit of a problem as no examples of the original nineteenth-century version have actually survived. There is, however, a copy at Drumlanrig Castle in Dumfries, home of the Scottish Cycle Museum, so Mave and I popped up to take a look.

Drumlanrig Castle is a huge house built in 1691 by the first Duke of Queensbury and it sits in a vast estate, all of which is now open to the public. The stable yard is where the Scottish Cycle Museum is housed, although it's not only old bikes that they have at the castle. You can also hire a mountain bike and take off round some of the MTB (mountain bike) trails on the estate.

The MacMillan velocipede.

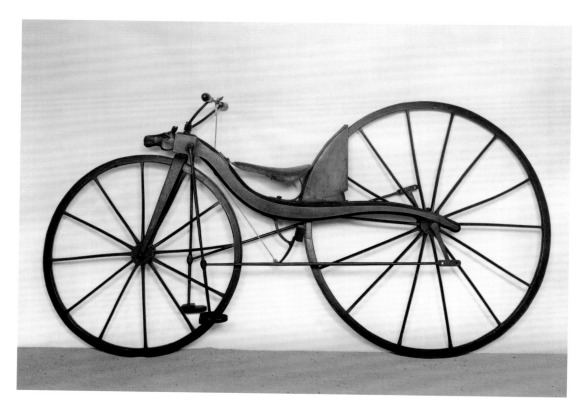

Drumlanrig Castle in Dumfries, home of the Scottish Cycle Museum.

Mave beat me in a race when I was on the MacMillan, but I had my revenge when I got my hands on the penny-farthing!

The old MacMillan wasn't really the machine for that, though, so we tried it out instead on a stretch of nicely surfaced castle forecourt. The bike took a bit of getting used to. There are no tyres on the MacMillan, and no suspension, just wooden wheels with metal 'tyres' on the rims. Because it uses cranks and levers, you don't push down on the pedals like you do on a bike with a chain drive. You have to sit on the bike, walk forward until you pick up enough speed to stay upright, and then carry on that 'sit-down-walking' motion, pushing the pedals back and forward. It was quite pleasant on the flat surface outside the castle, but I wouldn't fancy it much on a muddy forest path or charging down a mountain track.

Once I'd got the hang of it, we went for a bit of a ride on the estate roads, with Mave joining me on a penny-farthing from the museum. The roads were nice and smooth, except when I crossed a cattle grid: that sent a real shock up my spine and diddled around other bits that are best not diddled with when you're trying to film a TV programme! It's hard to believe that MacMillan rode his original velocipede from near where we were all the way to Glasgow. That's a distance of about seventy miles, which he completed in a day: the man must have had balls of steel! Unfortunately, when he got to Glasgow he knocked over a child and was fined five shillings for riding on the footpath. When he got home, so the story goes, he set his cycle aside and never rode the thing again.

The penny-farthing Mave was riding came along thirty years after my MacMillan and bicycle technology had come on a long way in the meantime. Although he was sitting really high on a big wheel, he was turning pedals that directly turned the wheel. But was he faster? We raced down the castle driveway and, as competitive as I am, I had no chance. He was miles quicker. When we came to a hill, though, it was a different story. It takes a very brave man to hurtle down a slope on a penny-farthing with no brakes to speak of. The penny-farthing does have a brake that presses on the tyre, and you can slow it down by 'back pedalling', but using the brakes generally meant that the penny-farthing rider took a 'header' and shot off the front of the thing, especially going downhill. Mave decided to fight against the pedals to control his speed and took it slowly. I didn't have any brakes either, but being lower down, I knew I could slow myself by scraping my feet along the ground if I had to. Mave would have needed legs six feet long to do that. Despite my advantage, the velocipede was still a bit hair-raising going down the slope. They told me I was doing about 11mph, but with no tyres, no suspension and no brakes to rely on, it felt like I was doing at least 25mph. It was fantastic. Coming back up the slope was a different story. It wasn't really much of a hill and you wouldn't think twice about powering up it on a modern bike, but on the MacMillan I was better off walking. Mave wouldn't have managed much better on his penny-farthing.

An array of traditional woodworking tools on display at Gayle Mill.

Left: You have to use a weird sit-down-walking motion to pedal the MacMillan – hard work.

Below: Mave and I study some plans to help us decide the best way to go about building our own version of the MacMillan.

The official name for the penny-farthing was the Ordinary Bicycle. It was called the penny-farthing because the large front wheel and small rear wheel reminded people of the large penny and small farthing coins laid side by side. It used tubular steel in its construction and was much lighter than a wooden cycle. The bicycle's inventor, Englishman James Starley, is often referred to as the father of the bicycle industry. Starley was not the only enthusiast working on penny-farthing-style, large-wheeled machines and these innovators established the use of wirespoked wheels, braking systems and rubber tyres (albeit solid rubber ones). Air-filled pneumatic tyres didn't come along until two Scotsmen – a vet named John Boyd Dunlop and a self-taught engineer called Robert Thomson – independently hit upon the same idea of wrapping a rubber 'balloon' around a wheel so that you could ride on a cushion of air. Thomson's tyre originally had the rubber tube inside a protective leather cover, while Dunlop is credited with having devised the first practical rubber tyre in 1888.

The Starley family never gave up on the cycle business and in 1885, James's nephew John launched his Rover Safety Bicycle. This was something that we would recognise today as being a proper bike. It had a 'diamond' frame just like most modern bicycles, pedal power with chain drive to the rear wheel and handlebars to steer the front wheel. The Rover Safety was more expensive than a penny-farthing but much cheaper than a tricycle, which was what posh folks preferred. There was no awkward or undignified

Clearing the filters
on the 'leet'
at Gayle Mill.

balancing to do with a tricycle and a gentleman could even take a lady passenger for a spin.

Cycles of all types had initially been playthings for wealthy enthusiasts, as only the upper classes could really afford them. Buying a new one was a bit like buying a luxury car today. Just like expensive cars, once the original purchaser had owned it for a couple of years, it was time for a new one and the old model could be picked up relatively cheaply – maybe even for nothing if it was damaged and regarded as little more than scrap. The less well-off would be on the lookout for such bargains because if a bike could be fixed, it could be used in races, and races meant cash prizes. A Newcastle man, George William Waller, won the world long-distance cycling championship on a penny-farthing in 1879 and earned a fortune competing as a professional bicycle rider.

At a time when most ordinary people never travelled more than twenty-five miles from their own homes, bicycles started to make day trips to the countryside a healthy and desirable thing to do. The middle classes – professional people who, unlike most factory workers, were allowed the occasional day off and could afford to buy bicycles – started making forays along roads that had long been forgotten by travellers now using the railways. Cycling clubs were formed and country inns that had previously served the stagecoaches now acquired a new lease of life. The Cyclists' Touring Club was founded in 1878 and hotels were so keen to do business that they offered special rates to club members. It meant a lot to a hotel owner to have the winged wheel emblem of the Cyclists' Touring Club on the wall outside. You can still see the cast-iron plaques on the walls of some country hotels today.

The cycle tourists weren't only good for the hotel trade; they were also good for the roads. Since rail travel had brought about the demise of the stagecoach business, there were fewer carriages and carts than ever on Britain's highways. Roads were not being maintained and had fallen into disrepair, something that the cycle movement set about putting right. They demanded good roads and quickly became such an influential sector of society that politicians dare not ignore them. Cyclists lobbied for better roads and, slowly, improvements were made. It was the cyclists, long before motorists came along, who ensured that Britain's road network was not allowed to deteriorate completely.

Mass manufacture drove down the price of bicycles and they became transport for the common man, and woman. The Victorians were very wary about women taking up cycling as they thought it was bad for a young lady's health, morals and reputation. Cycling entailed wearing shorter skirts that might expose a stockinged ankle or calf. It was deemed improper for a young lady to wear a knee-length dress and bloomers, baggy trousers fastened tight

Tony keeps a close eye on me as I sharpen the teeth on his circular saw.

around the ankle. Indeed, anything a woman might wear that was suitable for cycling was, in the eyes of many, liable to invite the unwelcome advances of the wrong kind of man. What would they think of Lycra cycling shorts?

It was even believed that cycling would be unhealthy for women in that it would damage their reproductive systems and that the leather saddles might even encourage ladies to indulge in the habit of masturbation. I know a lot of girls who go cycling, and I find it pretty hard to believe that that is the sport's major attraction for them ... As it turned out, cycling's detractors played right into the hands of those who were increasingly demanding reforms to give women the same standing in society as men. Girls went cycling and that, of course, simply encouraged more boys to do likewise.

All of this turned cycle manufacture into one of the boom industries of the late nineteenth century. There were only 100, 000 cycles on the roads in Britain in 1881 but within ten years there were 248 cycle manufacturers in Coventry employing almost 40,000 workers, and by 1906 these Coventry firms were turning out more than 300,000 machines every year. The cycle industry also expanded into car manufacturing, the industry that changed the world forever: John Starley's Rover Safety Bicycle spawned the Rover Company, which started producing motorcycles in 1902 and cars from 1904. The name lives on in today's Land Rover and Range Rover marques. The same is true of Triumph, which started life as the Triumph Cycle Company and also went on to produce motorcycles and cars.

The bicycle business was, therefore, very much an integral part of the Industrial Revolution. It remains a major industry worldwide with around a hundred million new bikes produced every year and a billion bikes in existence. Mave and I were about to make that a billion and one!

TROUBLE AT MILL

Back at Gayle Mill there were still a few jobs that we could get on with while we waited for the new turbine parts to arrive. Tony was on hand to explain a bit more about the mill and where the power comes from. They don't simply syphon off water from Gayle Beck to run the turbine. There is a whole system in place that would have worked pretty much the same way when the old water wheel was running – pretty much the same way for every water-powered mill, in fact. In order to make sure that they had enough water to turn the mill wheel, even when the weather was dry and the river was low, they created an artificial pond way upstream from the mill. The pond was topped up when there was plenty of water in the river and tapped whenever they needed more water down at the mill.

Immediately above the mill is a man-made waterway, a kind of aqueduct that is often called a 'race' but known as a 'leet' at Gayle Mill. The leet takes

Opposite: Trimming the end off a drive belt that had become too loose.

water from the river to a header tank at the mill, which in turn delivers a regular supply of water to the turbine. They can't have sticks and leaves or any other debris from the river going through the turbine, and there are metal grates that filter out such debris. These need to be cleaned, otherwise they restrict the flow of water to the header tank, and I helped out by raking muck off one of the grates. At one time the leet had a slight uphill section near the final grate; a drain hole at the bottom of the uphill section could be opened to let the water in the leet drain away, taking the accumulated debris with it. That was the Victorian solution to the problem but a later refurbishment of the leet managed to do away with it. Now it is a regular job for someone when the turbine is running.

There are always plenty of chores to do at a place like Gayle Mill and I don't mind mucking in, especially when I'm also being given the chance to learn completely new skills. One of those was making wheels.

> The two ends of the drive belt were joined to make a loop using open metal staples.

WHEELS OF FORTUNE

I needed two wheels for my MacMillan and they had to be made of wood. There are very few craftsmen in Britain today who can create a wooden wheel from scratch and I was lucky enough to be shown the ropes by Greg, who looks after the wheels and the carriages that are used by the Queen. His family have been working as wheelwrights and coachbuilders for centuries – Greg's been doing it for twenty years and no one knows more about wooden wheels than he does.

The process starts with the hub, which is made from a piece of seasoned elm. Elm tends not to tear or split as it grows, so you can be sure of a perfectly solid block of wood. That block is turned on a lathe to make it into a solid cylinder: the positions for the spokes are then carefully measured and marked up, and the spoke holes drilled out. These spokes are hand carved from square wooden rods of seasoned ash, and are planed one stroke at a time to give them exactly the right shape. This isn't a measuring process – it's one of the things that Greg said was right if it looked right. It's one of the elements of making a wooden wheel that is about judgement, feel and shape. That's what made me realise that this isn't so much a disappearing trade as a dying art. I did my best, and sat at the workbench for ages planing a little here and a little there. I know I got it right in the end – Greg wouldn't have been slow in telling me if I hadn't!

The holes in the hub (the hub mortices) are drilled at just the right angle so that the spokes can be hammered in to create the right pattern; pointing outwards left and right to distribute the weight that the wheel has to take evenly around the rim. The spokes have to be hammered in tight, but not so tight as to split the hub, at which point you're just about ready for the rim sections. There are usually half as many rim sections as there are spokes, with each section fitting on to two spokes. The rim pieces are carved and shaped based on a number of different templates that the wheelwright will have and butted roughly against each other. I was a little concerned by the number of little gaps – this wasn't what I was used to seeing when Mave turns out a piece of joinery – but Greg assured me that all was well.

> The staples are hammered into the end of the belt to grip it securely.

We then used a measuring wheel – the kind of thing that you see people rolling along the ground to work out distance – in order to measure the

outside of the wheel for the tyre. This was a metal tyre, made from a strip of mild steel. We bent the steel on a forming roller, then used a wheel to measure the inside of the tyre. It had to be a little smaller than the wheel, small enough that when it was fitted it would squeeze shut any gaps where the rim sections butted up against each other.

I welded it. I'm a dab hand at simple welding, so I was fairly confident about that part of the operation. When we offered it up to the wheel I couldn't believe that it would ever fit around the rim. It looked way too small but the idea was that we would now heat up the tyre in a bonfire so that it expanded. We'd then put it around the wheel where it would cool and contract to give a really tight fit, and squeeze shut those gaps.

The tyre needed just five minutes in the flames. We didn't want it so hot that it would buckle when we tried to pick it up and we certainly didn't want it to set our carefully crafted wheel alight! It had to be hot enough to scorch a piece of wood laid against it when it was sitting on the bonfire. When we took the tyre off the fire, we had to work quickly to make sure that it didn't cool prematurely. It was levered and hammered down onto the rim. A ladle or two of water cooled it off completely and forty-odd joints were squeezed into place, creaking and squeaking – 'talking' to us as it all fitted tightly together. Greg tested it with a few taps of a hammer and you could hear that it was tight as a drum.

That was a real creative experience, making something that is practical and quite beautiful out of a few simple pieces of wood. It's an impressive skill. Not so long ago you would go into town and have a wheelwright to look at your carriage, a blacksmith to shoe your horse and a pub down the road to take care of your driver. If your carriage wheel broke while you were out on the road, a wheelwright would come out from the nearest village with his tools and fix it for you. There were wheelwrights – the surname Wainwright means the same thing, 'wheel worker' – all over the country. Today there are probably fewer than fifty left.

SADDLE UP!

The other thing that I was going to need for my MacMillan was a good leather saddle. I had a look at how leather is made, starting with a piece of cowhide, and it was a thoroughly unpleasant business. The cowhide itself stank to high heaven, but there was worse to come.

The place where they used to produce leather, the tannery, was generally a building on the outskirts of town, and preferably downwind. Almost everything about the process creates the most disgusting stench. The tanners would soak the skins in water to clean them and scrape off any decaying flesh or fat with blunt knives. The skins were then soaked in urine or allowed to putrify for a few months to loosen any hair fibres, which were

also then scraped off with knives. The skin then had to be pounded with dung or soaked in a solution of animal brains. This was done to alter the chemical make-up of the cowhide, in order to help preserve it and to keep it supple. The favourite dung they used was from dogs. If you spotted someone walking the street carrying a basket and wearing one glove, you didn't need too many guesses to work out what he was up to. These were pure gatherers. Apparently the white dog poo was the most valuable!

Stinking cow hide,
freezing cold water
and disgusting
dog poo – keep smiling,
you're on telly!

Naturally, the TV people wanted me to have a go at curing the hide. Maybe they expected me to get carried away with the work, start rabbiting on and come out with something like 'By heck, much more of this and I'll have shit on me muscles.' I didn't give them the satisfaction, but I did suddenly appreciate why tanners tended to get married to other tanners.

Nowadays, we're all quite conscientious about picking up after our dogs so, thankfully, they couldn't send me out scouring the streets for the required tanning ingredient. They got buckets of the stuff from a nearby dog kennel instead. Unlike the Victorian tanners, the people at the kennels were glad to see the back of it.

The skins had to be soaked in a solution of dog poo and water, and kneaded constantly for up to two hours. I gave it a go using a tin bath. I had on heavy-duty rubber gloves – the kind you would use for handling hazardous chemicals – but the Victorian tanners wouldn't have had such a luxury. Any kind of cloth gloves, of course, would have been ruined and soaked through within seconds, so they just used their bare hands. In fact, they would even mash it up with their bare feet! It was a mucky job all right.

The tanning process actually takes months and as we didn't have that much time, thankfully, we were able to dispose of our tin bath concoction (properly – as hazardous waste) and head for the factory in sweet-smelling Birmingham, to see how the finest leather bicycle saddles are made.

Brooks of Birmingham have been making bicycle saddles since 1882. The firm was started by John Boultbee Brooks, who travelled to Birmingham from his home in Leicester with just £20 to his name, determined to earn his fortune. He started a business making horse harnesses and other leather goods when, in 1878, he was on his way to work one day when his horse dropped dead. They had me riding a horse to introduce this piece for the TV show. I'm much more used to riding something with two wheels than four legs but the horse was a lovely girl and she put up with me nattering away to the camera as we went down the street. Fortunately for all concerned, she remained very much alive all the way to the Brooks factory. The death of Mr Brooks' horse, you see, prompted him to borrow a bicycle from a friend in order to get to work. He found the saddle so uncomfortable that he decided to design his own, and the Brooks saddle was born.

The saddle we decided to make was one of the company's original designs, the Brooks Flyer Special. When I first saw it, it just looked like a bit of plastic with a few rivets in it, but this wasn't plastic, it was leather. It takes a whole day to make a Flyer Special. Brooks make 1,000 a day but they use Henry Ford-type production line processes, with each worker concentrating on doing one or two short jobs before passing the component on.

The first stage of the process is to form the metal frame of the saddle. You don't see much of this once the leather seat is in place, but the flexibility of the frame is what makes the saddle's 'suspension' work. Two springs, a right- and a left-turning one, are then twisted from a straight metal rod in a machine that heats the rod, twists it, cools it with water and pops it out as a fully formed spring.

That part was fun to watch but next I had to meet Lucas the leather expert. I was relieved to find that he didn't smell at all bad! Lucas showed me how the basic saddle pattern is pressed out of a thick leather sheet. The flat sheet is then squeezed and compressed between two saddle-shaped moulds. The machines that they were using in the factory were from the 1950s, doing the same sort of job the same sort of way that it has been done since the first saddles were made, so I didn't feel like we were cheating too much by not doing it exactly as they did in the 1880s. The Flyer Special hasn't really changed, hasn't really evolved at all. Then again, it doesn't really need changing – if it's not broke, don't fix it.

I trimmed off the excess leather around the mould with a very sharp knife and was then able to buff up the edges and make my saddle look the business. I admit I took a bit longer than the ladies who normally do this job and yes, I did hold up the assembly line, but they were very patient with me. They knew that I wanted to do a proper job and produce a saddle that was worthy of wearing that famous Brooks' stamp!

Eric was the man who oversaw the final assembly process – the last of around a dozen different jobs that were going on all over the factory – and he looked a bit nervous as I hammered in the copper rivets that fastened the saddle to the frame. It can't be easy for someone who takes pride in their work watching someone who looks like he could make a complete hash of it at any moment. He was as relieved as me when I finished the riveting, bolted the springs in place and produced a finished item that looked just the job. With a bit of suspension in the seat, my backside certainly thanked me when we finally got round to taking my MacMillan for a spin.

GET ON YOUR BIKE AND RIDE...

Before then, of course, we were back to Gayle Mill to put the turbine back together and fire up the tools to fashion the wooden parts of my new bike. There was a bit of metalwork involved as well but it didn't take too long to pull it all together once we got down to it. There was nothing else as complicated as those marvellous wheels that I'd made with Greg.

When I finally got to ride the bike, it went really well – a good deal more comfortable with the Brooks Flyer Special saddle than the MacMillan at Drumlanrig Castle. Even so, pedalling my MacMillan was a completely different experience from pedalling my Orange mountain bike racer. They are both state of the art for their time: it's just their times came at different ends of the factory phenomenon that completely changed the face of Britain.

Above opposite: I could easily outstrip Mave on our MacMillan . . .

Below opposite: . . . but, just like the original, there weren't any brakes!

FISH 'N' CHIPS

When was the last time you held a proper length of rope in your hands? Not many of us nowadays need to use rope on a daily basis. We don't need it for work and at home we even hang out our washing on plastic wires. Most of us probably only come into contact with rope through leisure pursuits – campers and climbers still use ropes, although they tend to be specialised ropes, and you'll use ropes if you go sailing. If you're wondering what rope has got to do with good old fish 'n' chips, the sailing reference is a big clue …

Most of us, then, don't have much of a clue about different kinds of rope and, unless you paid attention when you were at Cubs or Brownies, you probably aren't too good at tying proper knots either. All things considered, you might not think that you know anything about rope, but we still refer to it more often than we might think.

'A load of old rope' is a common phrase for something that is pretty useless or a bit dubious. The phrase stems from the fact that old rope is not as strong as new rope. It will not take the same sort of strain, or load, before it breaks. We've all heard someone say, 'he's a bit of a loose cannon' (I've heard it said about me more than once!) and a loose cannon aboard ship was one that had broken free of its restraining ropes. A three-ton loose cannon rolling around on deck could cause all sorts of trouble. You wouldn't want one of those trundling over your toes! We often say that someone in a new job is still 'learning the ropes', which comes from the way that sailors had to learn the specific use for every rope on a sailing ship. If you say that you are 'at a loose end', meaning that you don't have anything to do, you're describing yourself as a piece of rope. A 'loose end' on a sailing ship was an unattached rope that either wasn't doing its job, or had no job to do. You might have used the expressions 'tying the knot', 'getting hitched' or 'getting spliced' (again something that I've heard a few times recently), meaning 'getting married'. Hitching and splicing are ways of joining two ropes together to make one.

> We all know a lot more nautical ropey terms than we might first think.

And if you've ever 'let the cat out of the bag', meaning that you've blurted out a secret that means trouble for someone else, then you've used yet another ropey nautical term. The 'cat' in the phrase is the 'cat o' nine tails' whip that was used to punish sailors. It was kept in a bag and when it was taken out, it meant someone was in for a flogging. Why 'cat o' nine tails'? Because it was made from thick rope that had been unravelled at one end.

Around thirty-one miles of rope were used on HMS *Victory*.

The First Journey of "VICTORY," 1778.

Fred Cordier has been working with rope in Chatham for over fifty years.

The thick rope consisted of three thinner ropes wound together, and the three thinner ropes were each made of three strands. When they were unravelled, the 'cat' had nine tails. Knots were tied in the tails that would cut into the flesh of a sailor's back when he was being flogged.

Even if we don't realise it, then, we all have a connection with the ropes that were used for centuries aboard sailing ships. Ropes are still used aboard ships today, of course, the most obvious use being for mooring, but back in the nineteenth century a big, three-masted Royal Navy ship-of- the-line like HMS *Victory* needed more than just a mooring rope. The *Victory* needed around thirty-one miles of rope – twenty-six miles of that rope in the rigging. So where better to go to find out about rope than the birthplace of this famous boat – Chatham Dockyard?

DOWN TO THE DOCKS

Sitting on the banks of the River Medway in Kent, Chatham Dockyard was once the most advanced shipbuilding facility in the world. In over 400 years, it supplied the Royal Navy with 500 warships. In its heyday, the dockyard and its various buildings covered an area of over 400 acres with 10,000 men working on the site. While the dockyard itself closed in 1984, 84 acres of the original site is now run as a tourist attraction. Many of the historic buildings, meanwhile, are still in everyday use. One of these, The Ropery, is where the ropes for HMS *Victory* were made and they are still making rope the same way today.

It was in The Ropery that they explained to me about the 'rope' phrases that we all hear in everyday conversation. These lads were real enthusiasts and they certainly weren't scared of a bit of hard graft. When I rolled up with the film crew in tow, they were already at work and we were told to get a move on because they had plenty of rope to make that day! The Master Rope Maker, Fred Cordier (Cordier is a proper ropemaker's name – cord being rope – and shows that his family has a historical connection with ropemaking), had a team of four men working with him, making rope to order. He explained the whole process, starting with the Manila fibres.

Men have been making rope for around 28,000 years, although Fred was keen to point out that he's only been doing it for the last fifty years or so. Fred's prehistoric predecessors, having started using vines and creepers, soon saw how those wound around each other to make stronger 'ropes'. They copied that using fibrous strips from the stems of tall plants or grasses, twisting them together to make ropes. That, essentially, is what we are still doing to make rope today.

The Manila fibres come from the abacá plant, which is actually a kind of banana. Who'd have thought we'd be making rope from bananas? The abacá plant is commonly grown in the Philippines and those of you who

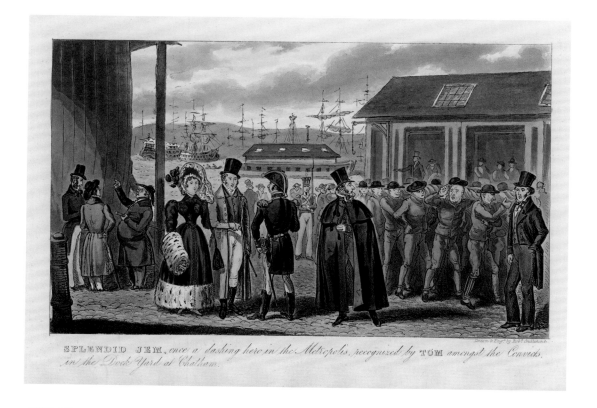

SPLENDID JEM, once a dashing hero in the Metropolis, recognized by TOM amongst the Convicts in the Dock Yard at Chatham.

can remember your geography from school will spot straight away that the fibres are named after the capital of the Philippines. The same fibres are pulped to make paper – hence Manila envelopes. I learned a lot here before I even got my hands on a bit of rope . . .

The fibres were imported into Chatham and were worked on site to make yarn. They had to be combed to separate and straighten them, were lubricated with whale oil to make them easier to work with and sometimes treated with preservatives before they were spun into yarn. At one time, spinning a length of yarn would have been a job for two or more men: one with the long Manila fibres wrapped round his body, walking backwards away from a spinning wheel that was being wound by hand by his mate. But by the 1860s (still well before Fred's time!) spinning machines took some of the heavy labour out of this task.

Once the fibres were spun, the yarn went off to the yarn house where it was soaked in tar to help prevent it from rotting. This didn't always happen with Manila as it was more naturally resistant to rotting than other rope-making fibres such as hemp, jute, sisal or flax. Manila could instead be treated with oils and preservatives prior to spinning which made the rope more flexible. Once it was dry and ready for rope making, the yarn finally made it into The Ropery building.

Rope has been made on site here since 1618, although the current ropery building dates from 1791. When it was built, it was the largest brick building in the world and it's still one of the longest. You don't really get a proper idea of its size from the outside, mainly because you can't actually see it all. Once you're inside, though, you can immediately see that it's a heck of a place. The first thing that you notice is the smell of hemp in the air. It's that dry, sort of musty, smell, like an old potato sack. Despite the fact that there's a window in the wall every few feet on both sides of the building and that there are electric strip lights hanging from the huge oak beams, it's still pretty gloomy inside. Once your eyes get used to the lack of light, you can see how the building stretches off into the distance. There are no steel beams or crossmembers holding this place together. It's all bricks and wood.

That, of course, means that there's a strong fire hazard here. If it looks dimly lit today, it would have been so much worse before electric light because they couldn't have candles or naked flames in the building. The dust from the hemp fibres would hang in the air and if some of it caught light, could cause a chain reaction that would send an explosion ripping through the building. The previous ropery on this site did, in fact, burn down. And they had a small fire in the existing building, too. Part of the floor had to be replaced and, this being a dockyard, they used whatever came to hand for repairs. The story goes that HMS *Victory* was being refitted at the time and surplus flooring from Nelson's cabin was used to repair The Ropery's fire damage. We saw for ourselves the patch of floor where the wood is different from the floorboards in the rest of the building.

So why is The Ropery such a long building? The answer is that the standard length for a British naval rope was 1,000 feet (305m) and you need a long building to wind ropes of that sort of length. The ropewalk, which is where the strands and ropes are laid for twisting, is 1,135 feet long (346m). Fred's lads travel the length of the ropewalk on bikes to save their legs – one reckons he's got up to 35mph in there!

TIME TO SPIN A YARN

Fred was keen to show me how the rope is laid. He needed to get on with our rope because they had another order to work on that day – there's no slacking in The Ropery! Fred showed me how the yarn comes to them wound on bobbins, or cops. These are mounted on a bobbin bank frame from which several yarns can be fed through the register, which looks a bit like a kitchen colander, and stops the yarns from getting tangled, to the forming machine. One of the machines we used there was the Maudsley Forming Machine, originally built in 1811.

Six or more yarns are attached to a hook on the forming machine. When the clutch is engaged – which they do by pulling a rope that runs the length of the building – a generator housed miles away at the other end of The Ropery kicks in. It supplies the power, via ropes and pulleys, that spins the hooks on

VÉRITABLE EXTRAIT DE VIANDE DE LA Cie LIEBIG.

2. — PLANTES FIBREUSES ET LEUR EMPLOI.
Production et emploi du manilla aux Philippines.

Reproduction interdite.   Voir l'explication au verso.

A stylish postcard showing Manila fibres in production in the Philippines.

the forming machine, twisting the yarns into strands. There were three such strands being twisted on the forming machine that I guided up the ropewalk. If the yarn on a bobbin runs out, yarn from a fresh bobbin on the bank can be fed into the register and is then drawn through to be incorporated into the relevant strand. Once the yarns are running through the register, they are travelling at quite a pace and spinning with a fair force. Fred carries a large, very sharp knife in a sheath at his side and explained that, when he first started as a ropemaker, all of the men used such knives. They used them, as Fred does, for cutting rope but Fred also said that, as a youngster, the older men warned him that if he got a finger tangled in yarn or strands that were passing through their machinery, he should cut his own finger off rather than end up with his whole hand or arm being ripped off. There was a battered old tobacco tin on a shelf in part of the rope works and Fred asked what was in it. He was told to leave it well alone. Naturally, as soon as the older men turned their backs, he had a look inside. It was full of dried-out old fingers!

Once the three strands have been twisted, drawn out along the length of the ropewalk and now looking like thin ropes, they are then twisted together to make a rope. When the winding machine is twisting the rope, the power from the electric motor – it was once a steam engine, of course – is used to do the winding. But because winding the three strands together means that they will end up as a rope that is only two-thirds the length of the strands, the forming machine is dragged down the ropewalk. There's definitely a lot of powerful forces at work here. I was standing on that machine as it moved along and it bore my weight quite easily. In fact, in order to maintain tension in the rope, the machine was dragging a selection of weights along behind it as well.

Opposite: The Ropery at Chatham – once the longest brick building in Europe.

Watching the yarn
zipping out through
the register.

The power that goes into it, however, is not the key to how the rope stays together. If you tried twisting a few strands of thread or string together, they would unravel as soon as you let the ends go: the threads would want to return to their original shape. The secret to making rope is to twist the yarn in one direction, the strands in the opposite direction to the yarn and the rope in the opposite direction to the strands. That way the different parts of the rope are fighting against each other to unwind in different directions and end up holding together instead.

Our finished rope was coiled and bagged up ready for delivery by the time we were ready to leave The Ropery. Before we left, we tested a section of the rope to check its breaking strain. The rope was laid out on the bed of a hydraulic 'rack' and wedged in place, the wedges gripping the rope tighter as the hydraulics stretched it tight. Then stretched it some more, and kept on going until the rope snapped. It didn't go all at once, but when the first strand snapped, with a noise like a gunshot, it was time to shut down the machine. Our rope was clearly strong enough for our needs.

TAKE ME TO YOUR LEADER

So what, exactly, did we want it for? Well, our rope was a three-strand laid rope, also known as a hawser-laid rope. You use a hawser aboard a ship, and the one we had in mind was an old trawler from Brixham in Devon. Brixham lies opposite Torquay on the southern side of Torbay and for many years it was the most important fishing port in the region, known as the 'mother of deep sea fisheries'. Limestone was mined in the hills around Brixham but the two main industries in the area have always traditionally been farming and fishing. The area at the top of the hill where the farmers lived was called Cowtown and the area around the harbour where the fishermen lived was called Fishtown. I like it when people keep things nice and simple like that. For a time, the area was also important for the red ochre mineral that was mined here. This had long been recognised as helping to preserve sails. It was boiled in huge cauldrons of seawater along with tallow, tar and oak bark and painted onto the sails while the mixture was still hot. The sails were then hung up to dry, the canvases having turned a sunset red colour. This was the inspiration for the old song 'Red Sails in the Sunset', which sounds a lot more romantic than 'Red Ochre Preserved Canvas in the Sunset'. Red ochre was also used to make paint that was used for rustproofing, the paint having been in invented in Brixham around 1845 and the paint works remaining in operation there until 1961.

It is, however, the fishing fleet that we are interested in. That's where one of the two primary ingredients for fish 'n' chips comes from, after all. I lent a hand with a few restoration jobs on a Brixham trawler called *Leader*. She is one of only six Brixham sailing trawlers still in existence, when at one time the largest fishing fleet in Britain sailed from the port. Launched in 1892, *Leader* is one of the biggest trawlers of her kind at around a hundred feet

The register looking like the head of Medusa with its snake-like yarns.

long and nineteen feet wide. *Leader* fished around the coast of Britain until 1907, when she was sold to new owners in Scandinavia. She remained as a working boat there until the 1960s, at which time she was used by the Swedish Cruising Club as a sail training vessel. In 1985, she found a new home on the west coast of Scotland, where she was used for holiday cruises, until she came back to Devon in 1996.

Brixham trawlers like *Leader* were fast and agile. Their two masts gave them the option of using up to eight sails, meaning that they could 'change gear' quickly, speeding up or slowing down as required. *Leader* was built at the A W Gibbs boatyard in Galmpton on the River Dart but was destined for the east coast, where William Robbens of Lowestoft had taken out a mortgage to cover the £1,100 cost of buying the boat. The records show that Robbens employed a skipper and mate who were paid a share of the profits. The first hand was on seventeen shillings a week, which was paid to his wife while he was at sea; the second hand earned thirteen shillings, to be paid to himself; and the boy was on ten shillings, paid to his mother.

Given the impact that steam power was having in industry and on the railways by the late nineteenth century, it might seem a bit odd that they were still building wooden sailing trawlers for the fishing business. Steam ships did exist, with their great advantage being that they didn't rely on the wind, but they also had to have specialist crew members – an engineer to run

The Maudslay Forming Machine, built in 1811 and still in use.

Opposite: On the other side of The Ropery from where we were working, a massively thick rope was being made, to be used for decoration at a golf club.

the steam engine and a skipper who knew how to handle a steam-powered boat. A steamboat also cost around three times as much to buy as a trawler like *Leader*, and these traditional sailing boats continued to be built well into the 1920s.

In the 1890s, while *Leader* was heading off to start her life in Lowestoft, there were 300 trawlers in Brixham harbour. Most of these were owned by families who made their livelihood from the boats. It was far from being an easy way to make a living. The romantic image of 'Red Sails in the Sunset' didn't really reflect the dangers involved in putting to sea: it was once estimated that a deck hand working on a trawler was three times more likely to die than a miner at the coalface. A skipper or his mate, because they worked longer hours than the rest of the crew, were at even greater risk – they were twenty times more likely to die than a man working in any other industry. Between 1879 and 1882, 235 of Grimsby's 4,000 fishermen were killed.

It was easy enough for accidents to happen when men were handling wet, slippery, heavy equipment on a heaving deck. If the weather turned really nasty when they were too far from port to run for safety, there were even more hazards to be faced. Ice forming in the rigging (a problem in the far north) had to be hacked away, to avoid making the boat top heavy and causing it to capsize. Even close to home, things could go disastrously wrong. Brixham's rocks, for example, have claimed countless victims over the years. In January 1866, a storm in the area forced many ships out to sea. Those struggling to find their way back in the dark couldn't pick out Brixham harbour, as the beacon that was usually lit on the breakwater had been swept away. The women of the town, so the story goes, grabbed anything they thought would burn well, including furniture and bedding from their homes. They piled it all up on the quayside to make a huge bonfire in the hope that their men would spot it and be able to head for safety. Despite their efforts, the coastline the next morning was littered with wreckage from fifty ships that were destroyed, with over a hundred men having lost their lives.

Those at sea didn't have much to help them if the ship went down and they ended up in the water. You might never have been on a boat or ship at sea and run through a lifeboat drill, pulling on a lifejacket, but you will probably have seen the cabin crew on an aircraft demonstrating how to use the life-vest that inflates when you hit the water, and has a light and whistle attached. Trawlermen working on boats like *Leader* had nothing like that, even though most fishermen didn't know how to swim. The lifejackets that were available in the nineteenth century were bulky affairs with cork floats attached. They were awkward to work in and, even if they had such things aboard, the men would choose not to wear them. They knew that if they were lost overboard they had practically no chance of being picked up. A lifejacket might keep them afloat, but not alive: in the North Sea in winter, for example, they could expect to survive for only four minutes before falling victim to hypothermia.

A moment of
contemplation
on the rope walk.

While working on board, the trawlermen had some very effective traditional protective clothing. Oilskins, capes or coats made from sail canvas soaked in linseed oil helped to keep out rain and seawater, while their ganseys kept them warm as well as dry. Ganseys were jumpers knitted to patterns that had been around since the sixteenth century and originated on the Channel Island of Guernsey. They were heavy and closely knitted to help them repel water, tight around the neck and cuffs to keep out the wind and short in the sleeve to stop them getting caught up in the gear aboard ship. The complex patterns were knitted from memory and passed down from mother to daughter as they made ganseys for successive generations of their family's fishermen (although men also knitted). They represented ropes, anchors and herringbones that were familiar to everyone in the fishing communities. Slightly different patterns would be used in different areas, and you could tell where a fisherman came from by the pattern on his gansey. Some families had their own patterns and might even incorporate the fisherman's initials in the design. If nothing else, it helped to identify his body if he was washed up on shore.

It's little wonder that sailors and fishermen have always been such a superstitious lot. I'm not one for strange superstitions myself, although I know that a lot of motorcycle racers have their own little rituals that they go through before a race, from putting their socks on in the right order to

When they are spinning, it's hard to take your eyes off the hypnotic hooks of the forming machine.

Opposite: Lining up our three strands ready for them to be twisted into rope.

praying in the loo. These fishermen, though, really take the biscuit. Some wouldn't sail if they passed a nun, a rook or a cat on the way to the docks. If they saw a rat coming ashore from their boat (and most boats had the odd rat or two) they wouldn't sail in case the rat was leaving a ship it knew was going to sink. They didn't like to whistle in case they whistled up a gale. Some simply wouldn't set sail on a Friday. Knives and forks could never be crossed on the galley table. The list is pretty much endless.

It was bad luck to have a woman aboard your ship. Women still played a vital part in the fishing industry, though, scouring the coastline to collect mussels or limpets to use as bait if the men were line fishing, and gutting and cleaning the catch when it was landed. They also worked on building the boats and mending the nets. If it was a family-owned boat, the captain's wife would be the business manager, taking care of all the paperwork while her husband was out at sea.

Women weren't allowed aboard ship, but boys were. Apprentices as young as eleven were taken on, first as cooks, then as deck hands, and these youngsters had to be tough. Not only did they have to put up with the cramped conditions and hard work aboard a trawler, but they also had to put up with the other regular crewmen. These would most likely be rough types at the best of times and very unpleasant when they had a drink inside them. Drink? When they were out at sea? Most definitely. Sensible captains might insist on a sober crew but, more often than not, hard drinking went hand in hand with being a trawlerman. Even when they were out in the fishing grounds of the North Sea, on a trip that might take them away from home for eight weeks, they needn't have worried too much about running short of booze and 'baccy'. 'Bumboats', also known as 'coopers', would accompany

Right: Cutting free the finished rope using the knife borrowed from Fred.

Opposite: The rope, rolled and tied ready to be packed in a bag for delivery, was a hefty bundle – so heavy that I could barely lift it.

A trawlerman wearing old-fashioned oilskins.

You could tell where a trawlerman came from by the pattern on his gansey.

the fishing fleet. They weren't there for the fishing. They were there for the fisherman. They sold everything from rum, whisky and tobacco to coffee, tea and saucy playing cards. Crews paid cash, traded part of their catch or, if they were really desperate, they might hand over some of their own boat's gear, hoping that they could get away with telling the boss when they got back that it had been lost overboard. There were times when a couple of apprentices were left in charge of the trawler while the crew boarded the bumboat to make merry. There were also occasions when apprentices were beaten so badly by other crew members that they died and the murderers simply dropped the bodies over the side, listing the apprentices as 'lost overboard'.

Like nineteenth-century factory workers, the trawler crews worked up to eighteen hours a day. They lived in cramped conditions below decks with no more space per man than was needed to bunk down. Storage for sails, rigging, nets and the fish was far more important. Before there were trawlers, boats that set out to catch fish in bulk used long lines – sometimes miles long – that might have up to 5,000 baited hooks attached. Fishing with nets was limited, partly due to the difficulty of hauling a large enough net through the water. Two boats might be used, each towing lines to hold the mouth of the net open wide enough to trap a decent quantity of fish. The Brixham trawlers were to change all that. These boats were fast and powerful, and able to deploy enough sail to haul large nets. A forty-foot-wide wooden beam was used to spread the mouth of the net with boards or vanes

at each side, forcing it open while also working with the weighted lower edge of the net to stir up the sea bed and frighten more fish into the trap. By the middle of the nineteenth century, an average day's catch for a trawler in the North Sea fishing grounds might be a ton of fish – mainly haddock but also plaice, whiting, turbot, brill and cod.

ICE ICE BABY

The trawlers developed in Brixham were soon to be found operating from ports all around the British coast, and especially from the east coast harbours that worked the North Sea fishing grounds. Their great advantage was that they were fast enough to get their huge hauls back to shore while the fish was still fresh. The other problem had always been how to get the fresh fish to the big inland towns before it all started to smell like something that died a week ago – which it probably had done. The trawlers were fast, but that wasn't much good if everything then had to be loaded onto a horse and cart. From the middle of the nineteenth century the railway network was able to help solve the transport problem on land. It was soon possible for fish that was landed in Grimsby in the morning to appear on a plate in a London restaurant the same evening – though only if it arrived fresh and could be kept fresh, even in the scorching heat of summer.

The answer was to pack fish in ice. Every fishing port had an ice house that would be stocked up from local rivers or ponds during the winter, the blocks of ice separated with straw or sawdust to stop them freezing together. The ice house at Barking in London could store up to 10,000 tons of the stuff. An ice house had no windows and thick walls to keep any sunlight that might hit the building from transferring the warmth of its melting rays inside, but storing ice could never be entirely successful. Ice was even imported from Scandinavia, but that, like storage, made it very expensive. What was really needed was a way to make fresh ice whenever you needed it, at whatever time of year, whatever the weather was like.

By 1756, a Scottish medical doctor and chemist called William Cullen had demonstrated how a liquid in a vacuum would first boil, then freeze. Research chemist Mhairi Matheson agreed to stage an experiment for me, based on the public demonstration given by Cullen that led to the development of artificial refrigeration. Mhairi was eminently qualified to do this. She had even made a molecule – benzodiazepine. I've never made a molecule, so I left Mhairi in charge. She explained that this experiment is the principle on which our modern fridges are based. We had a glass bell jar, the sort of thing that wouldn't look out of place covering a stuffed parrot, with a tube coming out of it. The tube was attached to a hand pump and Mhairi had me cranking away at it for ages without much result. It was only when I told her it was her shift that she plugged the tube into an electric pump!

It was shortly after that the whole experiment went pear-shaped. I had

Above opposite:
I put in some proper
hard graft aboard
a trawler, hauling
in the net.

Below opposite:
Heading home to
get our catch to market
still ocean fresh.

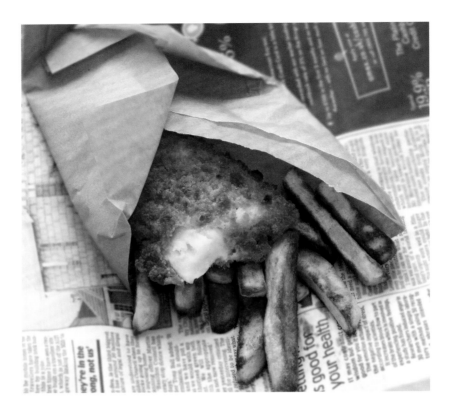

Fish 'n' chips is still one of Britain's top takeaways with more than 10,000 chippies nationwide.

been wondering why they had made us wear protective glasses for the experiment. We were only making a spot of ice and filming it for the telly, after all – what could possibly go wrong? The answer came when the big bell jar suddenly exploded. Actually, it imploded, but there was a heck of a bang and a fair few shards of glass flying around. By the way Mhairi screamed, I could tell that, even though she had done this experiment a hundred times, this had never happened before. I didn't scream, but the words that came out of my mouth are not the sort of thing you want to hear on telly and certainly not something a gentleman would ever be heard to utter in front of a lady. Unfortunately, I got such a shock that I forgot, for a moment, that I was a gentleman.

Undaunted, Mhairi fetched another bell jar and we had another go. I wondered what William Cullen thought when he had a few of these mishaps? It must have happened to him when he was trying to perfect his experiment. I guessed he must have just kept going, so that's what we did too – with an even sturdier bell jar.

When the pump evacuated all of the air from the jar, the water started to boil – at room temperature. Nature hates a vacuum, you see, so the water wanted to expand to fill the vacuum and the only way it could do that was to

BRIXHAM.

An impression
of the Brixham boats
and their 'red sails
in the sunset'.

evaporate. Water usually needs to be heated in order to boil and evaporate but because it had no external heat or energy source, the water used energy within its own molecules. The evaporating molecules of water took energy away from the water in the beaker, leaving the remaining water molecules with less and less energy. When molecules run out of energy, they grow cold. Eventually, the water freezes. Once ice could be created at any time of year, it meant that everything travelling by rail could be delivered fresh – not only fish, but also meat from a slaughterhouse and vegetables from a farm. Ice became cheaper to buy, meaning that fishing boats could afford to use more of it and stay out at sea longer to bring in bigger catches.

DO YOU WANT SALT AND VINEGAR WITH THAT?

There was definitely a demand for the fish – more so than ever before. Seven years of famine in Ireland between 1845 and 1852, when their potato crops were destroyed by blight, led to mass emigration, with thousands of Irish weavers arriving to work in the mill towns of mainland Britain. The Irish Catholics ate fish on Fridays and demand for fish in the second half of the nineteenth century soared.

Part of that demand was down to the way that fried fish was sold from stalls in the street. The fish was covered in batter to seal it, making it last longer and helping to stop it from smelling. By the early 1860s, it was reckoned that there were 300 fish fryers in London. They didn't yet offer you chips with your fish, though. Chips appear to have been invented by the French during a fish shortage, when street vendors cut potatoes and fried them instead of fish. It was a delicacy that soon caught on in Britain, especially in the north where Oldham and Leeds were thought to have had a fish 'n' chip shop for every 400 people – pretty much one chippy on every street corner.

Nowadays we have all sorts of fast food – Chinese, Indian, Malaysian, burger houses, you name it – but the chippy is still one of Britain's favourite takeaways. There are something like 10,500 fish 'n' chip shops across the country. There are only 1,200 McDonalds and 350 KFCs. Around 80,000 people work in chippies and the industry is thought to be worth around £1.2 billion annually, serving up 300 million portions.

I like to think I made that 300 million plus one, when I tucked into some fish 'n' chips while watching the restored *Leader* put to sea. A lot of people had volunteered their services to get the old girl shipshape again, and they had benefitted from a £170,400 Lottery grant. Leader didn't leave her berth in quite the same way as she would have done when she was new. You can't just fling up a few sails and set off from the quayside – a sailing ship needs a bit of room to manoeuvre under sail power – so trawlers like *Leader* were towed out into more open water. They used steam-powered tugs for that job, and before steam power the sailing boats were towed by gigs. These were fast

Opposite: Plenty of rope and hard work in evidence aboard the *Leader.*

rowing boats with six strong men at the oars. They competed to get to boats coming in to harbour, either to put a pilot on board whose local knowledge allowed him to steer the ship to safety through treacherous sandbanks or rocks, or to tow the ship to its berth. The fastest boat got the job, and the fee.

When *Leader* finally set sail, she had no need of a gig or a tug. Nowadays she has a six-cylinder, eight-litre diesel engine tucked away below decks, which gives her plenty of power to manoeuvre. When she unfurled her sails and cut the engine, *Leader* looked just like she would have done when she was heading for the fishing grounds over a century before. There are a few slight differences – below decks is no longer crowded out with smelly fishermen and their gear, and they no longer haul a ton of fish aboard each day. Instead, *Leader*'s decks hide comfortable bunks for twelve guests and five crew members, and a large saloon where everyone can eat in comfort, their meals cooked on a gas stove in a fully equipped galley. There are hot showers, two toilets (they call them 'heads' on board), a generator supplying electricity to sockets so that you can charge up your mobile and, naturally, all of the most modern navigation aids.

Mr Robbens' Lowestoft crew would surely love it – no fishing, just sailing for leisure and pleasure!

Leader looking just as she did when new – but with modern secrets lurking below decks!

THE
GARDEN

A scythe is a heck of a tool when you see one up close. The blade is razor sharp along its cutting edge and curved like a scimitar sword. The scythe's cutting edge might be on the inside of the curve, while the scimitar's runs round the outside, but that didn't stop it from being used as a weapon.

Back when the local landowner needed to raise troops to help form an army, the peasants who worked on his land had to become fighting men. They wouldn't be armed with expensive swords – they would have to provide their own weapons. Truth be told, anyone who had a scythe really didn't need a sword. The scythe's shaft (or snaith) is between five and six feet long and when it was used as a weapon, the blade (or chine) might be attached so that it stuck straight out from the end of the snaith, giving it a reach of at least eight feet – far enough to persuade anyone waving a sword at you to keep his distance.

It's little wonder that the traditional image of Death, the Grim Reaper, is a cloaked and hooded figure carrying a scythe. The scythe represented the way that the Grim Reaper stalked through the darkness of the night harvesting, or reaping, souls. That was the scythe's day job – harvesting crops, that is, not souls. When used for gathering crops, the chine would be attached to the snaith at right angles, forming a giant 'L' shape with the cutting edge on the inside. When the scythe was held ready for use in two hands, using the grip at the top of the snaith and another halfway down, the chine would be parallel with the ground. It's a good word that, isn't it – chine? Say it out loud and it sounds just like the noise a scythe makes as it slices through long grass. The scythe wasn't only used for harvesting crops, you see. In the days before the lawn mower, it was the tool used by gardeners to mow the lawn.

The proper technique for mowing with a scythe, and I was schooled by an expert so can describe this with some confidence, is to swing the scythe from right to left with the blade staying parallel to the ground. The aim is not to cut a huge arc of grass in front of you, as you might at first think – well, I did, anyway. The way an eighteenth-century gardener would have done it would be to swing the scythe as he walked forwards, cutting a small strip of grass on his right, then tipping the cut grass off the blade to his left, on an area of lawn he'd already mown. That made it easy for someone following on behind (I'd be following at a very safe distance) to pick up the cuttings. The mower was more likely to work his way round in a circle and finish in the middle of the lawn than try to move up and down in straight lines.

The cutting edge of the scythe blade was paper thin and razor sharp.

Apparently, experienced scythe men could do all sorts of tricks, including balancing one of these things on their chins – not me!

Unlike a lawn mower, the scythe worked better on damp grass.

Some scythes had a kind of s-shaped curve on the snaith that helped the mower to keep the chine skimming parallel with the ground. If they dug it into the earth it would not only chop up the lawn but it would blunt the blade. The cutting edge of a scythe used for lawn work would be paper thin, achieved by a blacksmith peening the blade – working the metal while it was red hot. A damaged blade might need re-peening, so what with loss of earnings and repair costs, the mower really had to get it right. Even for a skilled mower, cutting a lawn was backbreaking work and it would take a team of three or four men several hours to mow a large garden in front of a country house. It also had to be done early in the morning because the scythe did the best job while the grass was still damp with dew. The best job might well be a lawn shorn to just a few millimetres, bowling-green smooth.

Seems a heck of a lot of trouble and expense to go to just for a bit of grass, doesn't it? But that was the whole point. Any visitors arriving at your house would see your beautifully manicured lawn and be suitably impressed. A lawn looks nice, but it's not a productive thing. It's not an orchard or a field of corn or a cow pasture. It doesn't earn you any money. It is simply the owner of the house saying, 'This is my land and I have so much money that I can afford to grow grass here even though it is not a cash crop and I have to employ men to keep it looking in tip-top condition.'

BRITAIN IN BLOOM

Prior to the Industrial Revolution, gardens were for the rich but, as it did with almost every other facet of life in Britain, industrialisation, the coming of the factories, steam power and the growth of the cities, changed the nation's gardening habits. People from all walks of life were encouraged to develop green fingers.

Botanists have been collecting and growing plants for centuries. It might seem like there is nothing more English than a rose, but the Chinese were collecting and cultivating them 5,000 years ago. The rose is, in fact, one of the oldest flowering plants, having been around for some thirty-five million years – long before there were gardeners around to do any 'dead-heading'. In ancient Greece, Aristotle was studying botany 350 years before the birth of Christ and explorers were collecting plant specimens from all over the known world. When exploration really came of age with sailing ships from Europe circumnavigating the globe in the sixteenth century, all manner of exotic plants found their way back to Europe. In 1580, adventurer Sir Francis Drake is credited with bringing the humble potato to Britain for the first time – a plant that had obvious commercial value in that it would become a staple part of our diet. Where would we be without chips? Other plants were brought back by plant hunters purely because they were so beautiful or unusual. In 1656, the rhododendron, a common sight in so many of our gardens, was introduced to the UK from its home in the European Alps.

There was money to be made in finding useful vegetables, like the potato, or transporting plants like the tea plant from China to India to create a whole new agricultural industry. But it wasn't only farmers who were interested in new types of plant. Scientists were always looking for new species in order to learn about their properties and perhaps develop medicines from them. Botanists were passionate about studying plants from all over the world from a purely scientific point of view. It took time and effort to bring specimens back to Britain from the farthest reaches of the planet and sadly most of them died along the way. Those who set out looking for new species often didn't do any better than the plants they were after. David Douglas was a Scottish botanist who was sent to America by the Royal Horticultural Society as a plant hunter. He sent back hundreds of plants to Britain, including varieties of pine trees that helped to establish our timber industry: the Douglas Pine is one of many species named after him. Douglas didn't have it easy, though. Out in the wilds of Canada in 1823, looking for seeds and intending to take cuttings from fruit trees, he had climbed a tree to take a close look at some mistletoe when his guide ran off with his coat, his money and his notebooks! He survived many adventures exploring the west coast of America, including encounters with hostile natives, illness, starvation and falling into a raging river where he lost his rifle and all of his kit, leaving him stranded in the wilderness with only the wet clothes he was wearing.

Douglas met a tragic end in 1834 in Hawaii when, his eyesight failing, he was exploring the slopes of Mauna Kea, the highest mountain on the island – actually an active volcano – and fell into a bull trap. Domestic cattle that had gone wild were a problem in Hawaii and were hunted using pits that were

Brian Radam of the British Lawnmower museum was just the man to teach me all I could ever want to know about cutting grass.

Opposite: A Victorian illustration of a decorative Wardian Case.

Frontispiece

dug across paths the animals were known to take when foraging. Many of the hunters who came to Hawaii to help cull the animals were ex-convicts and there is some doubt about whether Douglas fell into the trap or was knocked on the head, relieved of some of his money, and pushed in. In any case, the bull in the pit put an end to Douglas's plant-hunting adventures.

By the middle of the nineteenth century, steam ships were cutting journey times enormously, although plants in transit still had to survive huge variations in temperature, being lashed by salt water blown across the deck by strong winds or being eaten by rats if down in a darkened cargo hold. Then in 1829, an East London doctor called Nathaniel Ward stumbled across the solution to the problems of transporting plants. Ward's home and surgery were in the Docklands area where the atmosphere was grey, gloomy, dismal and smoggy. He longed to grow delicate plants such as ferns in his garden, but the air quality simply wasn't good enough. The good doctor also had an interest in entomology, the study of insects, and was observing a hawk moth chrysalis when he made a remarkable discovery. He had put the chrysalis on some leaf mould in a sealed glass jar, hoping that he would be able to see the moth emerge. The moth died but the leaf mould came to fascinate him even more. Seedlings sprouted from the mould, including a fern of the kind that he had found so difficult to grow outside. Ward worked out that the plants were protected from the foul atmosphere inside the jar: the moisture in the leaf mould was evaporating during the day, then condensing on the glass when the temperature dropped in the evening and running back to be absorbed by the mould again.

Ward knew all about the difficulties of transporting plants around the world and decided to stage an experiment. In 1833, he built two strong wooden cases and planted in them a variety of grasses and ferns before sealing them in under glass. The cases were sent to Australia on the deck of a ship. The plants all survived the journey in good condition, as did some Australian ferns, never transported live to Britain before, on the return journey.

The Wardian Case became a feature of Victorian parlours, ferns and even orchids being grown in houses where this would previously been unthinkable. A plant hunter named Robert Fortune successfully used twenty-six Wardian Cases to send back hundreds of plants from China in 1843. Five years later Fortune caused a sensation when he disguised himself as a Chinese merchant in order to sneak out of the strictly controlled areas that foreigners were allowed to visit in China. He then managed to buy 20,000 tea plants – something that foreigners were absolutely forbidden to do – and 17,000 germinated seedlings, shipping them to India in Wardian Cases. Along with the tea, he hired eight Chinese tea growers who helped to establish the tea plantations in India.

A TOUCH OF GLASS

In a way, it's a quite surprising that nobody came up with Ward's idea a bit sooner. The Wardian Case was, after all, just a kind of portable greenhouse and these had been built in Europe since the thirteenth century, with the Italians using them to house exotic plants that explorers brought back from tropical locations. They called them *giardini botanici* – botanical gardens. In the sunny, warm climate of Italy, these greenhouses, no doubt, did their job just fine. In Britain, though, where it can get a bit chilly of an evening, keeping a greenhouse warm was more of a problem. In fact, for many years people thought that plants needed heat more than they did light. Gardeners kept plants in what they called 'stovehouses' – well heated outbuildings with thick walls and small windows. Needless to say, plants that gardeners tried to store over winter in stovehouses didn't do too well. Early attempts at greenhouses in Britain weren't hugely successful because gardeners struggled to keep the heat in them during the long winter nights.

Another problem with the idea of a greenhouse was its cost. Glass was pricey stuff to make and a glass tax that was introduced in 1746 during the reign of George II made it three times more expensive. That tax, described in the medical journal *The Lancet* as 'the most cruel a Government could inflict on the nation' because it was causing health problems by denying people light, was scrapped in 1845. Not only that, but glassmaking was becoming more efficient, and therefore cheaper, with the introduction of cylinder blown glass.

The way that glass was made prior to the introduction of the cylinder technique was to heat silica, commonly found in sand, in a furnace. Molten silica, mixed with other ingredients such as powdered lead, is what makes glass. A blob of the molten substance was scooped up on the end of a long, hollow iron tube. The glassmaker, or glass blower, then blew down the tube

Glassmaking 'chairs' at work around a furnace.

to turn the blob into a bubble. The bubble was enlarged until the glass was the desired thickness, then transferred from the blowpipe onto a solid pole called a punty. The glass was spun rapidly, forcing the bubble to reshape itself as a flat disc that could be around five feet in diameter. When this disc cooled, panes of glass could be cut from it.

Making cylinder blown glass was different in that once the bubble, or bulb, had been blown, it was dipped back into the furnace to add more molten glass. The heavier bulb was then reheated in a smaller furnace and blown again to make an elongated balloon. This was then swung gently from side to side to make it even longer, forming it into a cylinder. The cylinder was then allowed to cool, with the temperature controlled very carefully as it did so. Uneven cooling over the surface of the glass would cause the glass to crack. The ends were cut off and a slice was removed from the wall of the glass cylinder. The open cylinder was then fed into a furnace on a flat bed, the sides uncurled to fall flat and a sheet of glass was formed.

It's a beautiful process to watch and you can't but admire the skill of the glassmakers as they tease the molten glass – it wobbles around like jelly – into the shape they want. Like so many other industrial processes, however, it was hot, hard, dirty work and the conditions that the nineteenth century glassmakers had to work in were every bit as bad as those who worked in any other kind of factory. Glassmakers worked at least forty-eight hours a week in six-hour shifts – six hours on and six hours off. They worked Monday to Friday to keep the furnaces in constant production and over the weekend the furnace would have more raw materials added so that a new batch of molten glass was waiting for the first shift on Monday morning.

Glassmakers worked in teams called 'chairs' which, depending on what they were making, might consist of four men. If they were making a goblet, for example, the gaffer, the most experienced man, would be the one in charge. The servitor was his first assistant, the foot-maker was below him and the taker-in was the lowest of the low. The servitor would blow the first balloon to make the bowl of the goblet, and then hand the job over to the gaffer. He would be seated in the glassmaker's chair, which had long, sloping arms on which he could roll the blowing tube to keep the shape of the bowl, while also forming the base from a blob of molten glass brought to him by the foot-maker. A solid rod of glass called a pontil was then stuck to the base and the bowl cut off the blowing tube to be attached to the pontil. The gaffer would finish off the goblet using a variety of hand tools before the taker-in took it to the annealing chamber – the kiln where the glass could cool under controlled conditions.

Glass blowing remains a beautiful process to witness.

The glass houses at Birmingham Botanical Gardens.

The taker-in might also be sent out from time to time to buy jugs of beer. Blowing glass by a furnace, with other furnaces also churning out heat nearby, was thirsty work. Some factory owners even gave the chair a beer allowance to keep them going through the shift. It was in everyone's interest to keep up the work rate through the whole shift as glassmaking was piece-work, with the works' managers deciding how many goblets (or whatever the men were producing) should be made during a six-hour shift. If a chair produced twice as many, they would be paid twice as much. A gaffer's share of the proceeds could earn him up to £3 a week, while the others would get significantly less.

A glassmaker served a seven-year apprenticeship. It was traditional for fathers to pass on their skills to their sons, keeping the secrets of the glassmaker's trade in the family. Strangers seldom found their way into the industry: glassmakers closed ranks very effectively, to the point where their brotherhoods would pay a 'pension' to anyone who left the trade, on condition that he did not teach their skills to anyone other than a glassmaker's son. There were quite a few who were forced to leave the trade due to illness or injury – a glassworks where lead powder was being used and molten glass was being worked in furnaces was an unhealthy and hazardous place.

IT'S GETTING HOT IN HERE...

Dangerous they may have been, but Victorian glassworks were churning out glass faster and cheaper than ever before. With their furnaces burning day and night to produce high-quality glass and those in the ironworks working just as hard to produce precision metalwork, greenhouses came into fashion on a grand scale. Conservatories were attached to houses so that people could entertain in style in their 'indoor gardens', where tropical plants thrived. Wrought-iron frames, which could be made far slimmer and stronger than wooden ones, allowed light to flood in. Huge glass structures were built to create tropical or Mediterranean paradises at botanical gardens like the one that opened at Edgbaston in Birmingham in 1832.

Designed by John Claudius Loudon – a Scottish botanist, landscape gardener and writer – the Birmingham Botanical Gardens were established in 1829 on eighteen acres of land, formerly Holly Bank Farm. Three years of construction and planting, funded by the Birmingham Botanical and Horticultural Society, whose members' subscriptions provided the cash required, saw a range of trees and plants introduced to the garden. Many of these were donated by other societies all over Britain and Europe, including the London Horticultural Society (later to become the RHS) and the Berlin Botanic Garden, while a consignment of rare orchids came all the way from Brazil. Exotic plants need to be looked after in greenhouses and Loudon proposed a spectacular circular glasshouse, although his design was ultimately rejected because it would have cost too much. A simpler glasshouse was built to begin with, with others coming along later – the Tropical House in 1852, the Subtropical House in 1871 (eight metres tall

Opposite: Orchids were donated to the Birmingham Botanical Gardens all the way from Brazil.

so that it could accommodate tree specimens and also known as the Palm House), and the Terrace Glasshouses in 1883. The Terrace Glasshouses, which are now home to the gardens' Mediterranean and Arid collections, replaced the original greenhouses.

The gardens underwent a continuous programme of development with, for example, a bandstand being erected in 1873 and the Nettlefold Alpine Rock Garden coming along in 1895. I know the rock garden really well as I was involved in restoring it as part of the TV series. It was built by Backhouse and Sons of York, using 250 tons of millstone grit. James Backhouse, now he was a proper interesting bloke. He started a nursery business with his brother, Thomas, in 1815 when he was twenty-one and, as the business began to thrive, he married seven years later. Sadly, his wife, Deborah, died in 1827 and within three years, once his two children were old enough to be left with family, James set off on a ten-year missionary tour of Australia, Mauritius and Africa. As well as spreading the word, James also collected plant specimens to be sent home, helping to keep the Backhouse family business competitive in what was an emerging new industry.

The demand for new plants during the Industrial Revolution was such that nurseries began to spring up all over the country. Some sent out their own plant hunters, who could be quite ruthless in stripping valleys in the mountains of China – a collector's paradise because of the thousands of varieties available – of bulbs to send home. Ernest 'Chinese' Wilson, a highly respected plant collector who worked for Kew Gardens and had trained as

Opposite: Ernest 'Chinese' Wilson – born in Chipping Campden in the Cotswolds – was a prolific plant hunter who introduced 2,000 species to the UK.

Below:
The Rhododendron Walk at Birmingham Botanical Gardens.

J C Loudon pioneered gardens
for the people and was
heavily involved in designing
everything from armchairs to
the layout of entire towns.

an apprentice at the Birmingham Botanical Gardens, once gathered 18,000 bulbs that were lost on the voyage to Britain, so he returned to the same site the following year and dug up another 25,000 bulbs. He was caught in an avalanche in the mountains and his leg was crushed by rocks. Wilson had his porters splint his leg using the tripod of his camera so that he could be carried on the long trek back to safety. His leg never healed properly and, as he had been hunting for lilies, he called his injury his 'lily limp'.

As time went on, the nurserymen became better at growing their own stock and creating new hybrids in order to meet the ever increasing demand for garden plants. But just what was the cause of the gardening boom? The answer lies with men like John Loudon, whose many books about gardening promoted a style that was different to the very formal ornamental gardens and lawns that had gone before. His 'gardenesque' style introduced exotic plants displayed so that the planting could be admired from all angles and involved creating less rigidly defined flowerbeds. Loudon's gardening ideas generated a lot of interest amongst the green-fingered brigade, but he was also attracting attention with his ideas about town planning. He wanted more open spaces for ordinary people to escape from the grimy, polluted, cramped environments where they lived and worked, to enjoy the greenery of parks and gardens and breathe clean air. Loudon called for public parks in the cities and green belt zones around built-up areas where, as he put it, 'the exhausted factory operative might inhale the freshening breeze and find some portion of recovered health'.

PARK LIFE

Loudon was not alone in thinking that Britain's cities desperately needed parks and gardens. Captains of industry all over the country began to donate land where parks could be established, especially near schools or hospitals, for the benefit of the community. But that community still tended, in many cases, to be the same sort of people who enjoyed places like the Birmingham Botanical Gardens – basically, the middle classes. When the Botanical Gardens first opened, they were there for the enjoyment and education of those who had subscribed, namely the members of the Birmingham Botanical and Horticultural Society. This was not a place where a factory worker could take his family for a picnic in the sunshine.

Even when public parks began to appear during the course of the nineteenth century, there were strict opening times and strictly enforced rules: no walking on the grass; no ball games; dress codes that meant if the gatekeeper didn't like the look of you, you couldn't come in; and admission fees that meant the working man and his family probably couldn't afford it anyway. On Sundays, the only day when most workers actually had any free time, many parks were closed. Slowly, though, things began to change. When Regent's Park opened in London in 1820, it was a 'members only' establishment but by 1835 the general public was allowed in (if only on two days a week ... and they

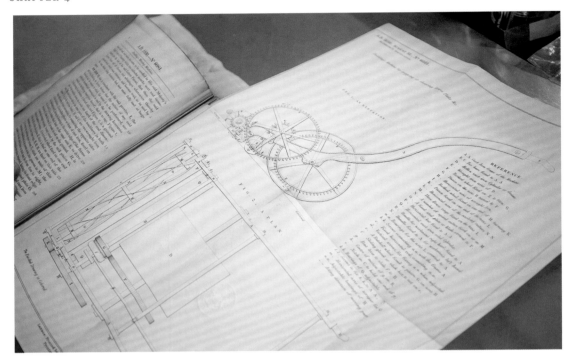

The original
drawings for the
Budding mower.

still had to pay). The first park to be laid out for use by everyone, funded by
the taxpayer and with no entrance fees, was Birkenhead Park on Merseyside,
which opened in 1847. As well as flowerbeds, lawns, paths to stroll along and
views to admire, there were boating lakes and sports pitches that the workers
from the local shipbuilding and ironworks could enjoy whenever they had the
chance. There were still plenty of rules that you had to stick to, as you would
expect in Victorian England: anyone found gambling, boozing or swearing
was asked to leave and would probably never be allowed back in again.

A park like Birkenhead needed a team of gardeners to look after it, just like
the teams that worked in the gardens on large country estates. Working as a
gardener at a big house was a far healthier option than working in a factory, but
the same kind of hierarchy existed. You might start work as a potboy at the age
of just ten – cleaning and repairing pots, spreading ash on paths, and following
along behind the under-gardener, picking up all the deadheads he had just cut
from a flowering plant. Once you had served your time as a potboy, if you had
kept your nose clean you might be promoted to under-gardener and start to
learn a lot more about gardening. Under-gardeners had to know about different
types of plant, what kind of soil they preferred, how much light or shade they
needed, and how to deal with weeds and moss in the lawn – basically everything
about the garden. Because gardens in different parts of the country can grow
some plants more successfully depending on how well suited the plant is to
the location, under-gardeners would aim to move every few years in order to
accumulate the knowledge that they needed to become a head gardener.

The head gardener was well schooled in the art of horticulture and would know the Latin names for the plants he was expected to grow, or that he recommended should be grown, in the garden. He would understand about soil types and drainage, the best place to site a greenhouse, the right time of year to tackle all of the jobs in the garden and how many men he needed to get those jobs done. He might not actually dirty his hands in the garden himself, but would give precise instructions to his under-gardeners and, when blooms or vegetables from the garden won prizes at the local show, he would take all of the credit. A head gardener would have to keep himself up to date with all of the latest developments, reading the latest journals in the evening after supervising his workforce all day. Gardeners made maximum use of daylight, working from dawn until dusk.

Head gardener was a position that would command some respect, yet the staff who worked indoors would still look down on those who worked in the garden and, even though a head gardener in the late 1800s might earn as much as £2 a week, the butler would still be earning more than him.

VEGGING OUT

The public parks and gardens of private mansions certainly helped to keep the nurserymen busy, but the massive interest in gardening was taking hold elsewhere, too. In the countryside, farm workers had once grown food for their families on common land but, as I found out when we were learning about how farm labourers became factory labourers, the common land was gradually taken from them under the various Inclosures Acts (see page 66). In 1845, however, The General Enclosure Act stipulated that land had to be made available to the poor in the countryside so that they could cultivate

Brian and I work out how to build our own Budding lawnmower.

what were called 'field gardens'. Very little land actually seems to have been passed back to ordinary people living in the countryside under this Act, but it did encourage people to start thinking about what very quickly came to be known as 'allotments'.

The allotment idea soon caught on in urban areas, too. One of the first cities where small patches of ground – Loudon reckoned that a quarter of an acre was sufficient to grow onions, cabbages, parsnips, leeks, beans and potatoes – were made available to rent as urban allotments was also one of Britain's most industrialised areas. Birmingham had been an important industrial centre since the sixteenth century, when metalworking developed there – the town being close to iron ore and coal deposits. By the middle of the seventeenth century, Birmingham had a population of around 5,000 people but a hundred years later this had grown to 25,000. By the beginning of the nineteenth century 73,000 people were living there and in the 1860s the number rocketed to a quarter of a million. Workers were flooding in to the city to find jobs in the factories and their living conditions were, for the most part, quite appalling. Sewage-ridden slum areas saw repeated outbreaks of smallpox and scarlet fever in the 1870s and 1880s.

Yet Birmingham was also responsible for establishing the cult of the allotment, with 'gardens for rent' available all round the most heavily developed areas of the city. In the 1830s, there were over 2,000 allotments being cultivated mainly by people who worked in the city's factories and shops. Edgbaston Guinea Gardens, taking its name from the price of the annual rent, is still there just two miles from the city centre, having survived the years of building developments that saw the city spread out around it. On parcels of land like these, people didn't simply grow vegetables; they also planted flowers. The flowers not only looked pleasing, but they attracted insects that were vital for the pollination of the food crops. Allotment gardeners became skilled at gathering seeds, storing and propagating their own plants, but the nurserymen could still rely on them for a fair bit of business. The biggest contributors to the growth of the nurseries, however, were those who had the chance to escape from the city streets to the suburbs. The owners of suburban homes with gardens became enthusiastic gardeners, keen to grow all sorts of plants, flowers, fruit and veg.

The voices of Loudon and others of influence were being heard by the town planners and local authorities, who had been tasked by the government to clear the streets of sewage and give city dwellers a decent living environment. Some industrialists, like the Cadbury family, took the opportunity when expanding their factories to build highly desirable homes for their workforce. The Cadbury company, who had been tea and coffee dealers, had expanded into cocoa and, famously, making chocolate. Like a number of other benevolent employers, the Cadbury family believed that a happy worker was a reliable and productive one. When they built their

Welding would not have been an option for Mr Budding, but sometimes you have to cut a few corners ...

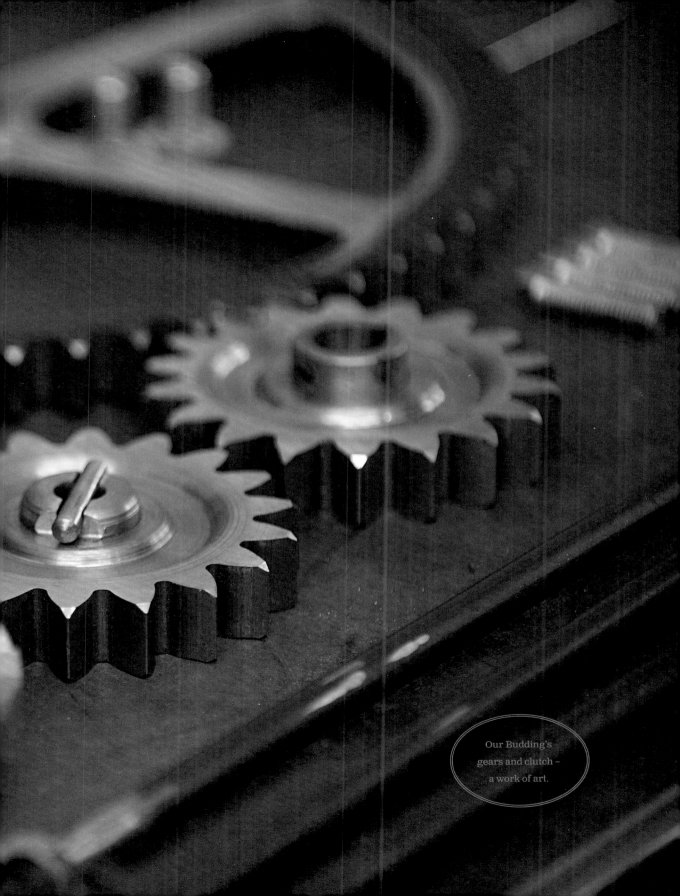

Our Budding's
gears and clutch –
a work of art.

new factory at Bournville in 1879, they also built houses for the workforce that had their own gardens, as well as open spaces that encouraged their employees to enjoy the fresh air during their free time.

ONE MAN WENT TO MOW

Towards the end of the nineteenth century, new housing projects were designed to allow for garden areas and tree-lined streets made for a far more pleasant living space. While larger houses in the suburbs, with big gardens, were affordable only by middle-class professionals and merchants, local authorities were also becoming involved, and the first council houses were starting to appear. These houses, too, were surrounded by gardens.

All of these new gardens included areas of lawn. The Victorians, who were mad keen on inventing machines to do all sorts of jobs, just had to come up with a way of cutting the grass that was more efficient and more mechanical than simply having someone stroll up and down with a scythe. That really did look a bit too medieval for the thoroughly modern Victorians. The man who came up with the first practical lawn mower was Edwin Beard Budding, who filed a patent for his grass-cutting machine in 1830, which is slightly before the Victorian era (she came to the throne in 1837), but by the time the lawn mower really caught on, it was her face on the coins and banknotes.

Born in 1796, Budding trained as an apprentice carpenter. He moved on to work on factory machinery and it was while working in a woollen mill that he got the idea for his lawn mower. The mill was producing cloth for guards' uniforms, so it had to have a perfect finish. A rotating blade was used to skim the surface of the cloth to remove any loose fibres and produce a smooth 'nap'. In fact, the nap would lie perfectly smooth in one direction but slightly rough in the other. They use the same technique in woollen mills today, especially when they are producing the green baize cloth for snooker tables. The wool is expected to have a smooth run and a rough run, where the ball will run faster or slower, and it has to be right when the world's top players can have a fortune in prize money riding on just one shot.

Above opposite: Once all the component parts were finished, it took Brian and me a while to assemble the whole thing in the right order . . .

Below opposite: . . . but we wasted no time in setting off to try it out.

Budding realised that the rotating blade could be used along with a flat blade to trap and cut blades of grass on a lawn. We took a look at the plans for his original machine and decided that, in order to see how well it worked, we would build our own. It took a fair amount of work but I had some lads helping me who knew exactly what they were doing. Budding would have been seriously impressed. They took his drawings and used CAD (Computer Aided Design) technology to recreate the parts that must have taken him forever to make. We visited the Science Museum in London to take a look at the earliest version of Budding's machine and work out how it was all put together. The tricky bit was the blades. The young engineers with their computer technology couldn't work out how Budding had attached the actual cutting edges to the rotating blade assembly. There didn't appear to be any riveting involved and it was too early for welding. It turned out that

the blades were pushed into slots and little metal wedges were hammered in to hold them in place. Once the metal had rusted a little, the blades were fixed in place for good. Clever, practical and not something you would come up with by using a computer!

The blades were turned by gears that delivered the power from a cast-iron roller at the rear of the machine. There was a crude clutch, actually just a long metal arm, that could be used to knock the gears apart so that the mower could be pushed across the lawn without the blades turning and ruining a cut pattern that had taken ages for the gardeners to achieve. With the mower, you see, the roller flattened the grass after cutting first in one direction and then, on the return journey, flattened the next cutting lane in the other direction. In this it differed from the nap on a snooker table as on the snooker table you don't have the stripes that mowing creates in the lawn. Getting the stripe pattern to look immaculate became part of the gardeners' art.

Budding's mower was a heavy beast. The cast-iron arms that formed the side frames were beautifully curved. Had they been straight, they would have worked just as well, but they wouldn't have looked as nice. Victorian engineering was as much about form as it was about function. The arms had grips at the end that allowed you to push the thing, but, because it was so heavy, there was another handle that swung out to the front so that another man could do some pulling – mowing the lawn was still a two-person job. As soon as we finished machining the last of the parts and assembled the whole mower, we took it out for a trial run. It worked a treat, shearing the grass very nicely and leaving stripes, even though the grass we were cutting was a bit damp. Fine for a scythe, but not so good for a heavy old lawnmower which tended to slip and skid a bit.

A lawnmower like this was no use for cutting the grass in the front garden of a small house where the lawn was only a few paces long, and these were expensive machines that would cost a working man a month's wages. Machine-cut lawns, however, became all the rage amongst those who could afford them. As well as building the machines themselves, Budding and his business partner licensed their manufacture to Ransomes who became one of the world's most famous lawnmower companies.

I've always had a soft spot for lawnmowers, as it was thanks to them that I first got interested in engines. As a kid I loved taking old Suffolk Punch motor mowers apart, making them work, then running them till they blew up so that I had to fix 'em up all over again. Hours of fun, although I wasn't that interested in actually cutting any grass. The tattoo I have on my leg – the flaming piston – is a piston from a Suffolk Punch.

We needed our lawnmower to be ready in time to help cut the grass the old-fashioned way in time for the new season at the Birmingham Botanical

Opposite: One man went to mow ...

173

Gardens. We had to have the rock garden sorted as well and my job there involved using a technique that was devised by garden designer James Pulham. As well as using natural stone in the rock constructions that were his speciality, he made the most fantastic grottoes, fountains and ferneries using a material that was known as Pulhamite. He would use rubble, old bricks and stones to create a basic structure and then cover it in a kind of cement that he mixed to achieve the colour and texture of natural stone. Pulham then moulded and modelled the cement, spreading it over his base material to make rocks that looked so much like the real thing, you wouldn't be able to tell the difference. Because Pulhamite was often used alongside real rocks, that was entirely the point.

I don't know if anyone could tell whether my efforts were the real thing or not, but the whole restoration of the rock garden and cascade (which is a Grade II listed structure) was done along with specialists called the Rock & Water Group. We were all proud that when the restored garden and cascade was officially opened by local MP Gisela Stuart, it was renamed the Diamond Jubilee Cascade.

Gardening has come a long way since the days when you needed a gang of peasants with scythes to mow the lawn. The average man now walks 220 miles behind his lawnmower during his lifetime and we all take it for granted that we have gardens outside our back doors, garden centres where we can drop in to buy all kinds of plants and public parks that are free for everyone to use. It's one of the most pleasing and unexpected legacies of the great Industrial Revolution.

Opposite: Our Budding gave us regimented stripes that they would be proud of at Wimbledon or Wembley!

COAL MINING

The show we were filming was meant to be all about coal mining, so what was I doing standing on top of a giant mound of clay in Yorkshire, up to my knees in muck and slithering about like Bambi on ice? I was making bricks, of course.

Most people, if they need to put right the garden wall that the wife backed the car into, just pop down to their local DIY warehouse and buy a few bricks – once they've had the car repaired. It was never going to be that easy for me, though. I needed special bricks, not standard house ones. I needed the kind that they used in the nineteenth century – a different size and shape from modern bricks. I needed the kind they used when they were building a beam engine.

GET THE ENGINE RUNNING

The beam engine was a steam-driven pumping machine, the first really useful steam engine. If you were to ask the average man-in-the-street who invented the steam engine he might say 'George Stephenson' because he's getting mixed up between his steam engines and steam trains. He might even say James Watt, because he knew that Mr Watt was very successful when it came to building steam engines for industry. But not many people you stopped would be able to tell you that Thomas Newcomen designed his steam engine in 1712, a century before Stephenson put his first locomotive on the rails and almost twenty-five years before James Watt was even born. His machine wasn't like the traction engines that I've been lucky enough to drive during the making of the TV show. It didn't go anywhere. It was permanently installed on site, pretty much a building in its own right.

Newcomen, from Dartmouth in Devon, was an ironmonger with an interest in all things mechanical. He looked at the ideas that had been tried by other inventors and engineers working on pumping systems and then added a few twists of his own, to create a piece of machinery that is a mechanical work of art. To understand how it operates, imagine a beam balanced like a seesaw on the top of a wall. Attached to one end of the beam is pumping gear that will lift water. This reaches way down into the bowels of the earth and is pretty heavy, so when the machine is at rest, the pump end of the seesaw is in the 'down' position. On the other side of the wall, attached to the 'up' end of the seesaw beam, is a giant piston. Below the piston, at ground level, is a boiler heated by a coal-fired furnace at the base of the central wall.

Opposite: An illustration of what is accepted as the first Newcomen steam engine at the Conygree Coalworks near Dudley in 1712.

Below: Collecting a barrowload of clay from the massive mound at the York Handmade Brick Company.

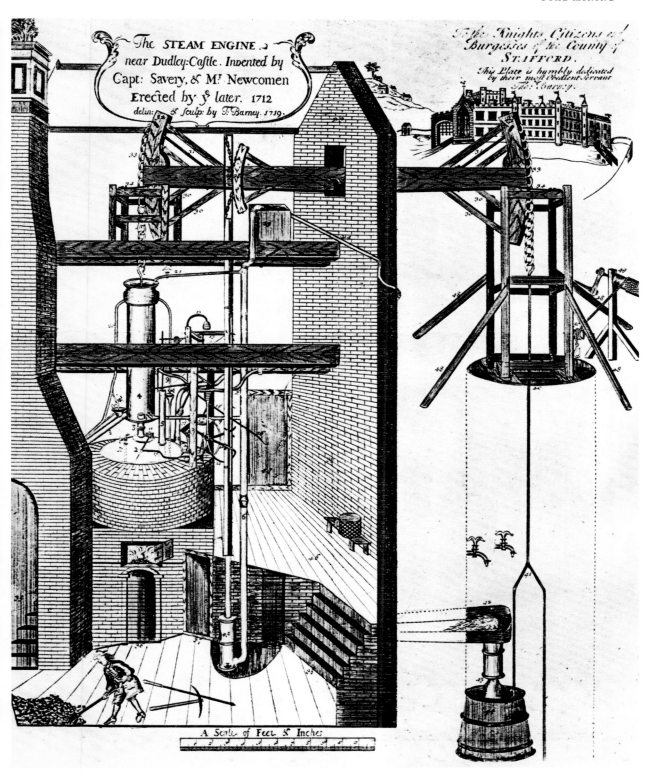

The STEAM ENGINE
near Dudley-Castle. Invented by
Capt: Savery, & Mr. Newcomen
Erected by ye later. 1712
delin: & sculp: by T. Barney. 1719.

To ye Knights, Citizens and
Burgesses of ye County of
STAFFORD.
This Plate is humbly dedicated
by their most Obedient Servant
Tho: Barney.

A Scale of Feet & Inches

When a valve is opened, steam is released into the piston's chamber. As the chamber instantly fills with steam, the valve closes just in time for another valve to open, spraying a squirt of cold water into the steam. The steam immediately condenses, contracting into a puddle of water at the bottom of the chamber. This creates a vacuum and pressure from the atmosphere forces the piston down into the chamber. The little puddle of water is ejected, the weight of the pump gear pulls the piston back up again, more steam enters the chamber, and the entire cycle starts all over again.

BRICK BY BRICK

The reason, then, that I was standing on top of a mound of clay was because I was collecting some of that muck to make the bricks we needed, to restore some of the brickwork on a beam engine. The whole process started with a barrow-load of very wet, sticky clay at the York Handmade Brick Company just outside Alne in North Yorkshire. They've been making bricks here for more than seventy years and, while they have the most modern kilns and processes to ensure that all of their regular products are spot on, the guys there offered to lead me through the way bricks would have been made more than a century ago. The brickworks, like most brickworks, sits right beside the raw material that they need. They dig the clay out of the ground on site and get to work with it. Actually, it's not quite that easy. The raw clay is heavy with water and they have to let it dry out, leaving it outside to weather like seasoning timber – the sun and the frost breaking it down until it is almost crumbly. Then they put the water back in again, but do so in a controlled way to achieve a mixture of the right consistency for making bricks.

This part of the process is called 'tempering' and is best done by a machine that mulches the clay up into a mixture of clay, sand, water and other ingredients (sometimes old pulverised bricks or even ground glass) depending on what colour the brick is meant to be and what it's going to be used for. Two centuries ago, this process would have been done by hand, or rather by foot. The brick makers would have bashed their mixture with clubs, turned it with spades and even trodden it with their bare feet – a bit like peasants treading grapes in France but without an end result that would leave you legless. Maybe I spoke too soon there. I had a go at mixing the clay with my shoes and socks off, and treading that mix, slipping around and struggling for balance, would have left my legs spent if I'd had to do it all day. This was a job that children often used to do, as their smaller feet were good at feeling for little stones in the clay that could burst when the brick was fired.

Fortunately, when we were filming, we had to rely on the old *Blue Peter* trick of using 'one I made earlier', because we needed far more mix than I could produce in the time that we had. I would have had to march up and down for days in the plastic trough we were using if I was ever going to get my mix to

Opposite: Sand is one of the things that is mixed with clay when making bricks.

the right consistency. The proper mix was available inside the brickworks and I was shown how take a portion of clay called a clot (about the size of a small loaf), dust it in sand and then 'dash' it into a mould (you have to dump it in hard to make sure you don't have any air bubbles in there). Then you have to trim off the excess, dust the top with sand, knock the clay out onto the workbench and slide it onto a drying tray. We were using a metal form, but wooden moulds were what would have been used in times past – they were often made from beech, because the clay didn't stick to it so easily. The reason the sand was dusted in the mould and on the clay was to stop it from clinging to the mould.

The guys who were working on special handmade brick orders made it all look so easy but once you have picked up a few dozen of those clots and dumped them in the mould, you start to feel it in your arms. The blokes who were showing me the ropes have arms like pistons and can turn out over a thousand bricks a day each. That's about the same as a brick maker would have been expected to do during a fourteen-hour shift a couple of hundred years ago. If he was working as part of a team, with one delivering clay, one cutting clots, one moulding bricks and a couple of others carrying and stacking, together they could produce 3,000 to 5,000 a day. This was piece work, so the more they made, the more they were paid: a brick maker in the middle of the nineteenth century would earn around four shillings for every thousand bricks he produced. A thousand bricks a day is some going, but to build an average-sized house might take 20,000 bricks. Even so, that's only a fraction of the four-and-a-half million bricks made at the York Handmade Brick Company every year.

The team at the brickworks had made a special mould for me that set my name in each brick, which was a nice touch – much appreciated! They had also made a batch of bricks ahead of time because the ones I turned out would need at least two weeks to dry. Believe it or not, the bricks I moulded each still had over a pint of water in them. If they were to go into a kiln like that, the water would heat up, expand and blow the brick apart. We didn't want that happening, especially as we were going to fire the bricks in a very special kiln.

Bricks are bulky, heavy objects that are expensive to transport. At one time, rather than shipping tons of bricks to a building site, the brick makers would make the bricks on site instead, using local clay. We decided to try to do it just like that, building a kiln in much the same way that we did when I was smelting iron for the filming of *The Boat That Guy Built*. The brick maker's kiln was called a clamp. We used old bricks to build thick walls, placed the bricks to be fired in an even pattern inside, then built the walls over to roof it all in. There was no mortar used, just a bit of clay plastered on the outside to stop up any gaps (there were gaps left intentionally at ground level to act as flues and allow air to be drawn in). We lit a fire inside the clamp,

stoking it with wood through a door. A small hole in the roof let the smoke out, although smoke was filtering out through every little crack it could find around the walls.

Job done. All that we had to do now was check that the fire wasn't burning too fiercely and that we had enough wood to keep stoking it. It would take at least ten hours to fire our bricks in this way: the more bricks there are in your clamp, the longer it will take. We had a few dozen bricks in ours, but when this technique was used a couple of hundred years ago, they would build a huge clamp that could fire around 40,000 bricks. Even a million bricks in a clamp was not unheard of! Some clamps burned for three weeks, some might take three months.

It had been a cold, damp day and it was very pleasant standing round, warming our hands by the clamp and supping a cup of tea. Inside the clamp, the temperature was several hundred degrees but outside it was like a big radiator. Then I heard a strange, dull, popping sound. Then another one. The lads from the brickworks had a little chuckle to themselves and when I asked what was going on they just shrugged and said, 'Clay must still have been a bit wet, Guy – that's your bricks exploding!' Fortunately, only a few of them went pop and when we returned the next morning to take a look at the end result, we had plenty to help with the beam engine job.

> The lads who make the bricks by hand can turn out over 1,000 a day.

I was a bit slow
as a brick maker,
but I did a lovely job!

ALL FIRED UP

The actual job of a beam engine was to pump water out of a mine. Flooding was just one of the hazards faced by the men working underground but it was also a major frustration for mine owners. They knew that they had rich seams of coal down there, but couldn't get at them if the tunnels and shafts kept filling up with water. And from the early part of the seventeenth century onwards, Britain needed all the coal it could get. The Great Fire of London in 1666 brought about legislation that prevented people from using the most convenient material for building houses – wood – not only because it was such a fire risk but also because the government was concerned about Britain's woodlands disappearing. Wood being burned as fuel meant that less wood was available to the government for the building of warships. So they thought they would preserve the forests by encouraging people to build with bricks and burn something else. The message was, 'burn coal not the forests' which is ironic, really, because the coalfields started out as forests.

A LONG, LONG TIME AGO...

Around 300 million years ago, vast tropical forests covered most of the earth's surface. It was a time when the first dinosaurs had yet to appear, although there were probably a few lizard-like creatures roaming around, some big enough that you wouldn't want to bump into one on the way home from the pub. Then there was a catastrophe, some kind of global warming event, and the forests died. They collapsed to form dense layers of decaying vegetation on the ground but were then flooded with water, creating huge peat bogs. Over thousands of years the peat bogs were slowly covered with

York Handmade
arranged for my bricks
to be personalized!
Nice touch, that.

layer upon layer of silt, sand and rocks until what had been a forest was now buried deep underground. The layers of rock and soil and water above pressed down on the old forest layer, compacting it and transforming it into what we now know as coal. Coal may look like rock, but it's actually organic, made from plants, which is why it burns. There's a basic rule of science that says, 'You can't destroy energy, you can only change it into something else.' The energy that a tree absorbs from the rays of the sun goes into creating the carbon-rich wood of its trunk. That energy is still locked away in the carbon of coal and in burning it, we create a chemical reaction that changes the energy, releasing it as heat and light.

Movements in the earth's surface, coupled with erosion, brought some of the coal seams to the surface. We know that people in Bronze Age Britain, about 5,000 years ago, realised that this strange black rock would burn: they used it on funeral pyres. The Romans burned coal in Britain apparently not only on domestic fires but also in industry, providing heat to dry grain and for iron-working. Coal, the stuff that fuelled the Industrial Revolution and made Britain great, had actually been working hard for Britain for quite some time.

Finding coal became more of a problem as time wore on. It didn't take long for coal deposits found on the sea shore to be used up and any of the black stuff that had appeared as outcrops on hillsides was then chased underground, miners tunnelling into the hillside horizontally, following the coal seam in what is called a 'drift mine'. The other early type of mine was a 'bell pit': here an outcrop might have been followed down into the ground, creating a shaft that was enlarged underground to form a coal cavern, with the whole excavation making a shape a bit like a bell.

These early mines could easily become inundated with water either running in from the surface when it rained or soaking in from the surrounding soil and rocks. If the mine went deep enough to reach the water table, there would be water everywhere. The water table is the area below ground level where water has soaked down through the soil and rock until it has reaches a level that is impervious. The porous rock above that level then becomes saturated. If you dig into that rock, the hole you dig will quickly fill with water. Areas of rock that hold groundwater in this way are called aquifers. The depth you have to dig before you find the aquifer can depend on the rock formations in the area, the time of year and the weather conditions. The one thing that you can definitely rely on is that water will get into a mine. Getting it out is then the problem.

At first, the problem was dealt with in very obvious ways. Mines were 'baled out' by bringing water to the surface in giant buckets, much as they did with coal. This, though, was a slow process that held up mining operations. Water was also drained away from the coal seam by digging tunnels or channels that allowed the water to run off towards another part of the mine, from

Opposite:
To be honest, I'm more used to handling spanners than axes, but we needed plenty of firewood.

Above opposite:
Coal dust was packed
in around the
new bricks to help
fire them.

Below opposite:
The new bricks
were laid in a pattern
inside the clamp to
try to ensure that the
heat spread evenly
around them all.

where it could drain away naturally or be pumped out of the mine. Pumping, with the pumps driven either by manpower, horsepower or even windmills, provided an ideal solution in that they could extract the water from the mine most effectively. But these pumps were never powerful enough to raise water from the deepest mines – until, that is, steam power came along.

The Newcomen engine could pump water out of a mine to depths of 300 feet, although his first engine, installed at a coal mine in Staffordshire in 1712, was only working to 156 feet. By the time Newcomen died seventeen years later, at least a hundred of his engines had been built in Britain and northern Europe. All worked on the same principle, but they had progressively larger pistons – one Newcomen engine in 1769 had a piston with a diameter of more than six feet – in an effort to find more power and pump water from ever greater depths. Newcomen's engines were not very efficient and they needed a lot of coal to keep their boilers going. This wasn't a problem at a mine as the boilers were simply fed low-grade coal that didn't have much of a market elsewhere. They did, however, allow the mines to go deeper, churning out the stuff that Britain needed more and more of as the years went by.

In the middle of the sixteenth century, it is estimated that about 200,000 tonnes of coal were mined every year. By the start of the eighteenth century that figure had risen to three million tonnes and more than 80 per cent of the coal mined in the world was produced in Britain. By 1800, production had risen to ten million tonnes. The railways, originally developed as a way of transporting coal, were sending steam locomotives thundering along the length and breadth of the country by 1850, gobbling up coal at a rate of a million tonnes a year. Steam power for factories pushed production

from Britain's 3,200 mines up to fifty million tonnes by the middle of the nineteenth century, with production peaking in 1913 at 288 million tonnes.

A lot of figures. A lot of big numbers. But what do they all really mean? You can't really imagine what 288 million tonnes of coal looks like, or how big a pile it would make. To put it all in perspective, I tried to figure out how much coal you would need to fill an average living room in an average house. Using anthracite, which is the glossy black coal most of us think about when we think of coal and which is also the heaviest coal, you would need to shovel about 60 tonnes into your front room to fill it up. You can work out for yourself how many front-room-sized hunks of coal went to make up the 288 million tonnes that were dug out from below Britain in 1913 alone. It's amazing that Wales, the Midlands and the north of England, which along with the central belt of Scotland is where most of our coalfields lie, haven't just collapsed. Yet the appetite for coal demanded that the mines keep on churning it out.

It's not hard to see why we needed so much. Our factories, our homes, our power stations and our ships – our island nation's vital lifeline to the rest of the world – all ran on coal. Ships of all types, from tugboats and river cruisers to battleships and luxury liners all used massive amounts. Everyone knows the tragic story of the maiden voyage of the *Titanic* in 1912. She was, at the time, the largest moving man-made object on the planet, but she wasn't that much bigger than her rivals and her consumption of coal wasn't that different, either. *Titanic* had three enormous steam engines – two piston, or 'reciprocating', engines and a steam turbine. Steam was fed to the engines from twenty-nine boilers that were heated by 159 furnaces, which explains why the ship burned around 600 tons of coal a day, and the journey across the Atlantic would have taken five days. The *Titanic* actually carried enough coal to make the return journey without refuelling. So six thousand tons of coal – that's a lot of living rooms . . .

Every chunk of coal that was shovelled into a furnace aboard one of our ships was supplied by men who laboured thousands of feet below ground and who had followed coal seams that stretched for miles – even miles out under the sea. Coal is still mined in Britain today, although there are only a fraction of the number of pits that there once were and miners now have machinery underground that miners in the nineteenth century could never have dreamed of. Back in those days, a miner had only a pickaxe to hack away at the coal. Given that he would be paid by the amount of coal that he dug out of his section of the seam during his shift, you'd expect that pick – the main tool that he used – would be big and heavy, to help him carve out as much as he could as quickly as possible. In fact, the miner's pickaxe was a good deal smaller than one that you might see being used by a navvy above ground. The men had very little room to work in and, if they were hacking out coal from a seam that was only eighteen inches high, they would have to work

Opposite: A rough coating of clay on the outside of the clamp was plastered on to plug any unwanted gaps.

lying on their sides. It was normal for a miner to spend all day on his knees because the roof was so low. In the damp conditions of the mine, this meant that almost all miners suffered some form of rheumatism in later life, just one of the many health hazards that came from working down the pit.

LIGHTING THE WAY

Apart from his pick, the miner would also need a candle to see what he was doing. There was no other form of lighting in the mines but the naked flame of the candle could be a deadly friend. Early candles were made from tallow, which is basically animal fat, so the candle could even be eaten in an emergency. But they were also smoky, didn't give much light and smelled awful. Candles moulded from wax that came from whale oil, or oil from plants, were more widely used by the nineteenth century as they lasted longer, gave a brighter light and didn't give off such a terrible pong. Anything that improved the quality of the air down the mine was a huge benefit.

A brighter candle flame, however, wasn't always a good thing. If a miner's candle suddenly flared it might mean that there was 'firedamp' in the air. Firedamp is methane gas – marsh gas created by decaying vegetation and trapped in the coal and rock many millions of years ago. If a miner came across a pocket of firedamp, he was in trouble. Methane is highly flammable when it mixes with oxygen in the right proportions: pure methane will not burn but firedamp leaking into the mine atmosphere at concentrations of

Opposite: There was a hole to keep the fire stoked and a vent at the other side to help draw in air.

Above: We checked the temperature using an electronic probe and you could certainly feel the heat building in the clamp.

195

less than five per cent would make the flame of a candle glow more brightly. At between 5 and 15 per cent the gas would ignite, sending an explosion ripping through the tunnels and chambers of the mine. One of the worst such disasters in Britain came in 1812 at the Felling Colliery in County Durham. A pocket of firedamp ignited, triggering a coal dust explosion that claimed the lives of ninety-two men and boys working in the pit. Some of the youngsters were only eight or nine years old.

This accident prompted the invention of the safety lamp. Three men were working independently on finding a way to provide miners with a light that wouldn't cause firedamp to ignite. William Clanny came up with a complicated solution that involved insulating the candle flame from the outside atmosphere in a lamp with water above and below it, air to keep the flame burning being pumped into the light chamber using bellows. It was clever, but it wasn't really practical for everyday use by miners.

George Stephenson came up with the idea of adapting an oil lamp: the flame was enclosed in glass, and the air flowed into the lamp, through vents in the bottom. Methane could get in and burn inside the lamp, but the flame could not 'burn back' to ignite gas in the atmosphere. The lamp was tall and slim to allow the gas to burn and rise inside the glass before escaping through perforations in the copper lid. The glass was surrounded by perforated metal to protect it and Stephenson's lamp became known as the 'Geordie Lamp'. Geordie is a pet name commonly used at that time in the North East for someone called George. Because it was such a common name in the area, anyone from Tyneside is now called a 'Geordie'.

Sir Humphrey Davy's solution was also to use an oil lamp. Because the Davy Lamp and the Geordie Lamp both came about at the same time, in 1815, there were suggestions that one had stolen the other's ideas. In fact, the two systems are really quite different. In Davy's lamp, the flame was surrounded by a wire gauze that absorbed the heat of the flame and spread it across its surface so that it was not hot enough to ignite the methane.

The new safety lamps soon caught on, and other versions were to follow. But they didn't eliminate the firedamp problem altogether. The gas could still be ignited by miners' picks sparking against rocks, for example, and there was an obvious danger when they were using explosives. Even so, the safety lamps reduced the risks immensely. The miners loved the lamps and the mine owners were delighted: an accidental explosion meant sealing off a coal seam and leaving any un-mined coal in the ground, which hit their profits hard.

Another advantage of the safety lamps was that their flames would burn a different colour if there was firedamp in the air, turning blue instead of yellow. The miners could then abandon their work until the gas was cleared,

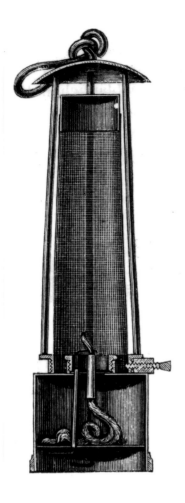
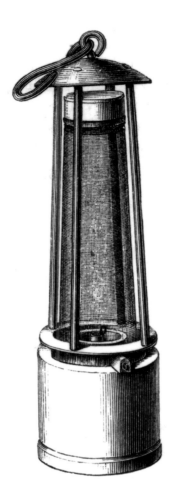

either by letting it escape through the ventilation shaft or being burned off by a very brave lad, known as 'the monk'. Draped in a long, wet, woollen cloak – hence the name – and with his hands and face wrapped in wet rags or leather, the monk would approach an area of firedamp with a lighted candle. If the gas, which was lighter than air, had accumulated at the top of a tunnel or gallery, the monk would crawl along the ground, where he would still be able to find breathable air and hold up a candle on a long pole to burn off the gas. If the gas simply flared and burned away, the monk would be okay. If it exploded, he probably wouldn't be so lucky.

Nowadays, mining companies can recover methane from mines and even use it on the surface, burning it to heat water in boilers so that the miners can have a good hot shower when they finish their shift. The nineteenth-century miner was afforded no such luxury. In fact, he was provided with nothing except the opportunity to work hard in a very dangerous environment. He

Cutaway and illustration of Sir Humphrey Davy's safety lamp.

had to supply his own equipment, which would usually have to be bought from the company store, and even employ his own team to recover the coal that he dug, install the wooden pit props used to hold up the roof of the coal seam and operate the wooden doors in the mine that were supposed to help ventilate the place.

The cheapest way to organise all of that, of course, was to bring in the family. The miner, also called a 'hewer', worked the coalface using a pick, wedges, a hammer and a shovel. He would shovel the coal into wicker baskets called corves that sat on wooden sleds.

The sled would then be towed out of the seam by his son, his wife or his daughter. The miner's youngest child (and children as young as four or five years old worked down the mines at one time) would be the 'trapper', opening and closing the wooden doors that were there not only for ventilation but also to help contain a blast should there be an explosion. Young children would also be used to sit and pump bellows to circulate air in the mine. The family team would probably have just one candle between them, so everyone except the miner would be working in the dark.

In 1865, an economist called William Stanley Jevons wrote a book called *The Coal Question*, which was all about when Britain's coal reserves would be used up. Although he wasn't too concerned about the conditions that existed down the mines, he did discuss how the temperature increased the deeper you went into a mine: 'in one Cornish mine men work in an atmosphere varying from 110° to 120° Fahrenheit ... ' (that's 43° to 48° Celsius) '... but then they work for twenty minutes at a time, with nearly naked bodies, and cold water frequently thrown over them. They sometimes lose eight or ten pounds in weight during a day's work.'

WORKING CONDITIONS

The Cornish mine that Jevons was talking about would have been a tin mine, and until a few years earlier conditions in a coal mine would be little different. Men worked alongside women and children, all practically naked. The work was particularly demeaning for women and girls. A woman who worked as a 'drawer' or 'hurrier' would tow a sled loaded with a wicker basket of coal by using a leather belt or girdle strapped around her waist. The belt would have ropes or chains attached to it so that she could crawl along (there being no room to stand up), dragging the sled behind her. In 1841, a Royal Commission was set up to investigate working conditions for children and young people in mines. Commission inspectors toured mining towns conducting fact-finding interviews and one such official, John Kennedy, interviewed eighteen-year-old Rosa Lucas in Lamberhead Green, not far from Wigan. Rosa worked as a drawer and had first gone down the pits when she was just eleven years old.

When asked what hours she worked down the pit, Rosa replied, 'I go down between three or four in the morning and sometimes I have done by five o'clock in the afternoon, and sometimes sooner.' So Rosa was normally

The clamp had to be kept going well into the night to fire our bricks.

I was well chuffed
with the finished product
the next morning.

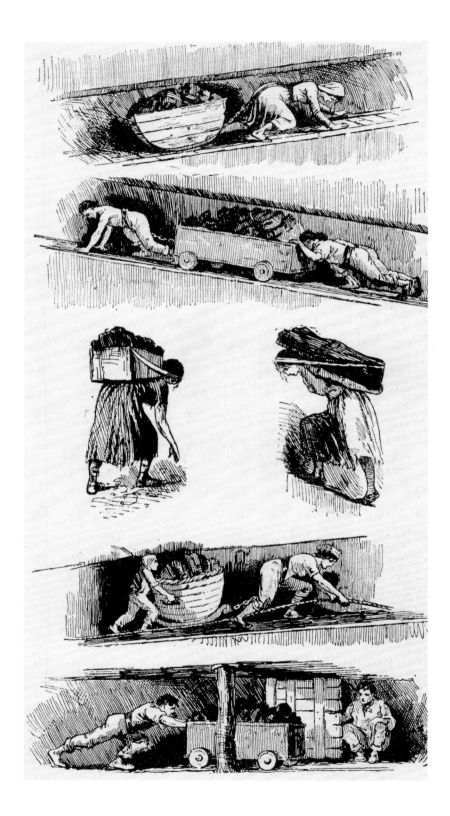

Entire families worked in the mines, enduring conditions that were quite appalling.

working at least a twelve-hour shift, and it was hard graft at that. She was asked the distance that she had to pull her load of coal and said it was 'twenty-three score yards in length'. A 'score' means twenty, so she was pulling her coal load for 460 yards, then pulling the empty sled back the same distance for the next load. Rosa said she was doing that eighteen times in one shift. That means she was crawling about, drawing her load for up to nine-and-a-half miles, every day.

Did she find the work hard? 'Yes, it is very hard work for a woman. I have been so tired many a time that I could scarcely wash myself at night.' At the time she was interviewed, Rosa was not working down the pit any more. She had been injured during a recent shift when 'a great stone fell from the roof on my foot and ankle, and crushed it to pieces, and it was obliged to be taken off.' Rosa lost her leg.

Not only did young women like Rosa (whose father had been killed in a mine accident) face the dangers of explosions, roof falls and flooding, if they were not thought to be working hard enough, an overseer would be on hand to administer a beating. Rosa identified a woman called Mary as being the one who beat the drawers and said it was done with 'a pick arm'.

The Royal Commission had been set up in response to the public reaction to an accident at the Huskar Colliery near Barnsley in 1838 when twenty-six children, all under sixteen years old, most under twelve and some as young as eight, drowned while trying to escape from rising flood water after a freak storm sent a torrent into their section of the mine. When the commission's report was published, there was an even greater public outcry, resulting in the Mines and Collieries Act of 1842. Not only were people appalled at the thought of women being used as beasts of burden, but Victorian morals were outraged at the thought of women working practically naked and seeing men doing the same. The subsequent Act prohibited all females from working in the mines. Boys were banned from working in the mines until they were ten years old and within a few years the lower age limit was raised to twelve.

While some were saved from the dangers of the mines, for those who remained working underground, conditions were slow to improve and miners continued to suffer ill health. Lung diseases caused by constantly breathing air laden with coal dust were common and it was rare to meet a miner who was older than forty-five. As bad as it was, breathing air full of muck and dust was better than having no air at all. Miners faced a constant hazard from 'black damp', which was sometimes also called 'choke damp'. Unlike firedamp, black damp was a silent killer, slowly reducing the oxygen content in the air until miners passed out and suffocated. Coal, you see, has a tendency to absorb oxygen once it is exposed to the air. It then gives out carbon dioxide. This, along with the miners breathing in oxygen-rich air and breathing out carbon dioxide, could lead to black damp creeping up on men working underground, without them even noticing. What they needed was something to warn them of the danger. But what could they use as an early warning system? The answer was … a canary.

ANIMALS AND BIRDS

Canaries have far more sensitive respiratory systems than humans, and cannot tolerate air that is no longer fit to breathe. If your canary keeled over and dropped off its perch, it was time to get out of that part of the mine until it could be properly ventilated. The canary, if it was given fresh air quickly enough, might even survive. From 1911, by law, all coal mines in Britain had to keep canaries to check for gas underground. They were still being used until reliable electronic detectors were introduced in the 1980s. The last 200 canaries were made 'redundant' from the British coalfields in 1986. They lived out the rest of their days as miners' pets.

The canary wasn't the only animal that was put to work down the mines. Pit ponies, generally smaller breeds such as Shetlands or Welsh Cobs, were used to haul wagons of coal, often working deep underground, and lowered down the mineshaft in harnesses. These ponies seldom saw the light of day. They would be reared in stables in the mine and start their working lives down the pits when they were three or four years old. Their underground stables were normally close to the surface where it was easier to supply them with fresh air, although the stable hands were careful that their ponies

Right: Coal mines were required by law to keep canaries to check for poison gas.

Opposite: Pit ponies became very attached to their handlers and became upset if they had to work with strangers.

were not left standing in a draught when they were off duty. That would be bad for the pony and these ponies had to be properly looked after. They had to have enough space in their stalls to stretch and relax their muscles after a hard day's work and they were fed on a healthy diet of hay and oats. Of course, what goes in one end of any horse comes out the other in a far less savoury fashion. That didn't improve conditions in the mines at all. Ponies, their straw, their food and their dung also attracted unwelcome guests into the mines, increasing the number of rats and cockroaches the miners had to put up with.

A horse working down a mine is as weird to me as a fish riding a bike. They are creatures that you naturally associate with running around in the fresh air, yet they were used in the mines from around 1750. At first, they weren't widely used because any kind of horse is expensive to run and needs to be well looked after if it is to be fit enough to do its job. Using women and children to haul coal underground was a cheaper option until the Mines and Collieries Act came along. After that, ponies started to make more sense.

At the largest pits, like the Grimethorpe Colliery, there would be around 300 ponies underground, and by 1913 there were an estimated 70,000 ponies at work in the pits. They might not have had what we would think of as a natural life for a horse, but they were seldom treated badly. They were, after all, a company asset and had to be cared for properly. The law looked favourably on them as well. By 1911, regulations insisted that there was at least one man allocated as a stable hand to look after every fifteen ponies in the mine. Ponies were also required to have protection for their heads to stop them being injured on tunnel roofs or joists, and they had to have blinkers to protect their eyes. It wasn't obligatory to provide miners with hard hats and safety goggles until the 1950s!

The pit ponies would normally have the same handler every day as they tended to get upset working with strangers. The miners were really fond of their canaries and ponies, and the animals shared the hardships and dangers that their human colleagues faced. Two weeks before Christmas 1866, an explosion in the Oaks Colliery near Barnsley killed 350 men and boys, along with forty pit ponies.

The pit ponies were allowed out once a year or so when the mines were closed for holidays, but they didn't really cope well with that. They weren't used to open paddocks, grass, trees and a huge sky above their heads and some were traumatised by the wide-open spaces. This became a real problem when the great British public, famous for being horse lovers, kicked up a fuss in the 1950s on discovering that pit ponies were sold off for slaughter at the end of their working lives. That working life might be anything from four to ten years, depending on the pony and the work it was doing. The idea that the ponies were simply worked until they were of no further use and then

Above opposite:
The ponies were stabled underground and seldom, if ever, went out above ground during their working lives.

Below opposite:
The animals were generally very well cared for as they were regarded as company assets ... and the miners loved them.

'got rid of' caused an uproar. After that, ponies were 'retired' to fields near their pits, but they needed a great deal of TLC to help them settle in to their new lifestyle. Sadly, many suffered from the same sorts of lung disease that afflicted the miners they had worked with. Few enjoyed long retirements, though some lived on to a ripe old age.

The last pit pony to retire from a British mine was Robbie, who worked at the Pant y Gasseg drift mine near Pontypool for five years up to 1999. He spent the next ten years in happy retirement at the National Coal Mining Museum, where he died in 2009 at the age of nineteen. It was there, at the old Caphouse Colliery, now part of the museum, that we filmed for the TV show and I learned so much about the lives of the miners who provided the fuel that turned Britain into the world's first industrialised nation. Without coal, there would have been no factory boom. It's been estimated that we would have run out of sites where watermills could operate by around 1830.

Coal is still mined in Britain today. According to the UK Coal Authority, there were thirty-five surface mines and thirteen underground mines still operating in England, Scotland and Wales in 2010, producing around eighteen million tonnes of coal and employing 6,000 workers. It's a far cry from mining's heyday at the beginning of the twentieth century, when one in five British workers were employed in the mining industry. Over the years, the high costs involved with mining coal in Britain made many of our pits uneconomical, even in pits where there were still substantial amounts to be dug out. Cheaper imports and the fall in demand as industry switched to oil or electric power led to the drastic reduction in the output from British mines. Even while there is talk about the high price of coal possibly making long-closed pits viable once more, there is also talk about further pit closures. Either way, there will certainly never be a return to the bad old days down the pit.

All in all, I think I'd rather do my digging above ground.

THE
HOLIDAY

There aren't many of us in Britain who can honestly say that they have never had a holiday. Even if it's only a few days away walking in the hills (I'd go for the mountain biking option there, I reckon), paddling on a beach or doing a spot of sightseeing, most of us manage to take some time off. Most people that you meet nowadays, in fact, have been abroad for a holiday, sunning themselves and having fun in places like Mallorca or Cyprus, or even further afield in Florida or Thailand. When you are off on holiday, once you've sorted out that day-before-you-leave passport problem, suffered the delays and battled through the crowds at the airport, found your missing suitcase, hunted out your hotel room, had a cup of tea and are finally strolling along with the sand between your toes on the beach, probably the last thing that you'll be thinking is that you owe your holiday to the British aristocracy and the Industrial Revolution. Seems ridiculous, doesn't it?

But you do.

TOUR DE FRANCE (AND ITALY, AND SPAIN, AND...)

At one time nobody really took holidays at all. Working-class people didn't have any time for holidays – at least, not a proper leisure-time holiday. A holiday actually meant what the word said: it was a holy day, when work might be set aside, as on Sunday, to spend the day at church, reading the Bible or otherwise praising the Lord. Holy days, holidays, were religious festivals like Christmas, but even at Christmas not every worker was automatically given the whole day off. In times past, the only people who actually had any real leisure time were the upper classes.

The aristocracy in the seventeenth century spent a great deal of time on sporting pursuits such as hunting, shooting, gambling and horse racing. Thoroughbred horses were then, as now, very expensive investments and only the seriously rich could indulge themselves and show off how rich they were, by owning a racehorse. Few people, even the rich, put up with the discomfort of travelling any great distance, but within their own counties the nobility would certainly want to be seen at all the right social gatherings, which generally revolved around their sporting activities. Knowing the right people was, after all, how you maintained your position in society but to make sure that the right people wanted to know you, you had to be able to talk about the right sorts of things. I like to think that I can chat with most people about lots of different things – not just trucks, motorbikes and Lancaster bombers. I enjoy finding out what interests other people and it's always good to listen to someone who knows what he's talking about. You can learn a lot when you've got your listening head on. To be able to make polite conversation with top-drawer people in the seventeenth century, however, you had to have a proper education. You had to to show that you understood

Right: Young gentlemen studying Italian art during their European Grand Tour.

Opposite: Getting to grips with another steam engine, this time a magnificent Showman's Engine.

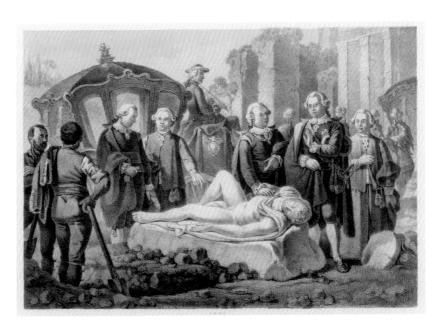

AT SCARBOROUGH.

about art, architecture, music, culture and horsey sport. That was what they chatted about at social gatherings. Other things – like business and politics – would be discussed by men only in rooms full of pipe smoke.

You won't be surprised to hear that they didn't have any Internet in those days, no TV documentaries, or even any public libraries or museums. The British Museum in London didn't open until 1759 and it was the first national public museum in the world. So, as part of their education, it became fashionable for young men (young ladies didn't need to be quite so well educated) to go to Europe to see great works of art and classical buildings at first hand. This became known as the Grand Tour. Young men would cross the channel to France or Holland (depending on who we were at war with at the time), then either hire or buy a coach (coaches if they were travelling with servants and a cook as well as their tutor/guide), or take a boat up the Seine to Paris, or up the Rhine to Basel. In Paris they might have lessons in French, dancing, fencing and riding.

To see works of art, most of which were held in private collections, these young men would be carrying letters of introduction to show that they were on a scholarly journey. They would be shown around grand houses stocked with treasures they would otherwise never get the chance to see, and perhaps even be invited to stay for a while: the very rich enjoyed showing off their collections and knowing that they would be talked about in high society when their visitors got back home. From Paris the travellers headed south to Geneva, then across the Alps to Italy where they visited Florence, Venice and Rome, and maybe even ventured as far as Naples to study music. The whole trip would take many months, sometimes even years, and the 'Grand Tourists' would ship home crates of souvenirs; not the wooden lizard, glass gondolier or Mount Etna snowglobe that you might find nowadays, but crates of paintings, sculptures and statues that would decorate the stately homes of England – something else for people to chat about at social gatherings.

There are plenty of reminders of the Grand Tour still around today. The name is where the GT letters on the back of a car came from. A proper GT, or Grand Tourer, is a car that can comfortably cover long distances at speed. The Grand Tour tradition continued right up to the latter part of the nineteenth century, sewing the seeds for the development of organised tour companies. It's also where the phrase 'travel broadens the mind' came from, the Grand Tour being a real learning experience. The young men who returned from their Grand Tour, if they managed to avoid being set upon by bandits, getting caught up in any nasty European wars and survived any stormy sea crossings, were far more sophisticated specimens than when they left.

Above opposite:
Victorians enjoying the sea air at Scarborough, the first seaside spa town.

Below opposite:
The magnificent Royal Pavilion at Brighton.

SO NEAR, SO SPA

Travel, then, was seen as a good thing, helping to promote a healthy outlook and a robust constitution. Taking this attitude to heart, the upper classes began to visit spa towns, rejuvenating the old Roman spa at Bath and establishing new ones such as Tunbridge Wells, Epsom and Harrogate, where the properties of the mineral waters were found to be good for the health. One seventeenth-century Dutch visitor to Epsom wrote that 'Epsom is a very famous and much visited place, very pleasant, and that because of the water which lies not far from there in a valley, which is much drunk for health reasons, having purgative powers ...'

Naturally, the new health fad didn't lead to the rich giving up their other pursuits. It's no accident that there are racecourses at Epsom, Bath and pretty close to every spa town. If people with money were visiting, then there was clearly money to be made in the spa business and there were plenty who wanted in on the act. Around 1620, a woman called Elizabeth Farrow discovered spa waters flowing into the sea at the North Yorkshire harbour town of Scarborough. The town was soon promoting itself as a rival to Harrogate, with the added advantage of refreshing sea breezes to perk up jaded socialites. Scarborough can lay claim to being Britain's first seaside resort, although it was well known as a market town for its trading fair – the Scarborough Fair from the famous song – for centuries before it became a holiday resort. By the 1660s, Dr Robert Wittie was recommending not only the mineral water at Scarborough but also the sea water as a cure for just about everything. Wittie was quite a well-respected physician and the author of *Scarborough Spaw; or a Description of the Nature and Virtue of the Spaw at Scarborough in Yorkshire.* Medical men who saw fortunes being made in spa towns inland weren't slow in realising that they could just as easily promote sea water as a health cure. Some recommended that it should be drunk with milk or honey, while others prescribed the drinking of it straight, three times a day after meals. These 'doctors' sound like complete chancers to us nowadays, but if you try drinking sea water – and I'm not recommending it – you are liable to be sick and the 'purgative' effect was one of the things that people in those days thought was doing them good, cleaning out their systems.

BRIGHTON ROCKS

In 1750, Dr Richard Russell, from Lewes in Sussex, published his *Dissertation on the Use of Sea-Water in the Diseases of the Glands, particularly, the Scurvy, Jaundice, Kings-Evil, Leprosy and Glandular Consumption.* Catchy title, eh? Russell reckoned that the sea water from Brighthelmstone was particularly good for the health and prescribed it for his patients, building a large house nearby where they could stay while undergoing treatment. When he died in 1759, the house was let to visitors, including the Duke of Cumberland. The Duke was visited in Brighthelmstone – by now more usually called Brighton by the Prince Regent, who later became King George IV. He had

a summer palace built in Brighton, the Royal Pavilion, with the royals adding to the allure of what had become Britain's most fashionable seaside resort. The Royal Pavilion was built in stages over a number of years and completely redesigned between 1815 and 1822 by John Nash to resemble an Indian palace somewhat like the Taj Mahal. But the more conventionally elegant buildings of the period, along with a seafront promenade, soon turned Brighton into the place for anybody who was anybody (or wanted to be somebody) to be seen.

Only a few years before, if you weren't a fisherman, a trader or a smuggler, there would have been no point in your visiting a place like Brighton, but by the end of the eighteenth century, wealthy visitors had turned it into a

We had to seek special permission to erect our helter skelter and steam-powered gallopers on the promenade at Llandudno.

The "Worthing Belle" leaving
Brighton Pier.

Paddle steamers
delivering visitors
to the seaside needed
piers where they
could dock.

thriving resort. They came not only to drink the sea water, but to bathe in it. They didn't go for a swim as we would nowadays. The 'swimmers' literally 'took a dip', again under doctor's orders, as being plunged into sea water – the colder the better – was guaranteed good for your health.

Other seaside towns soon blossomed in the same way: Margate, Eastbourne, Bognor Regis, Bournemouth and, the place where King George III first tried sea bathing in 1789, Weymouth. In the north, Blackpool began its transformation into Britain's Mecca for the masses although, like all of the other resorts, it began as a destination for the upper classes.

This is how the English nobility came to have such an influence over your annual holiday. Only the rich had the time to travel for leisure – London to Brighton by coach, even once there was a well-surfaced road, took nine hours – but they took with them their servants, who had plenty to gossip about with their friends and family when they got home. Ordinary people were well aware of the goings-on at the seaside resorts, they simply never had the chance to visit them … until the coming of the age of steam.

Even for the wealthiest holidaymakers, taking your luggage and servants with you was an expensive business. Rather than have an entire entourage travelling in a convoy of coaches, some heading for a holiday in Margate took to sending their staff by boat. The grain barges bringing cargo from Kent to London regularly made the return journey empty and their owners saw an opportunity to make money, offering cheap passage for those who did not require luxury accommodation.

Arriving at a seaside resort by boat, whether it was Margate, Southend, Brighton or any number of other resorts, especially once paddle steamers cut the sailing times and provided a reliable service, became a desirable and affordable option for the less well-off. Middle-class professional people and wealthy merchants were increasingly able to take time out for relaxation, and they followed the upper classes to the coastal resorts. Transferring passengers from the steamers (which had to anchor in deep water off the beaches) to small boats that struggled through the breaking waves to the shore, could be a very undignified business for image-conscious passengers. The answer was to build landing stages, or piers, that stretched out to the deeper water, allowing the steamers to berth safely and the passengers to disembark without getting their feet wet or losing their breakfast.

PIERS OF THE REALM

The first piers were built at Margate, Deal, Herne Bay, Southend, Brighton and Great Yarmouth. As the seaside holiday boom developed, the wooden, later iron, structures stuck out into the sea at every major resort. By the 1870s, Britain's coastline bristled with piers – two new piers were being built every year – but they weren't only used as landing stages. The pier became an extension of the promenade with the added excitement that you could actually walk out over the water. Swimmers could jump or dive off into the deep water and anglers could cast their lines from the pier. Later, the pier was also to develop into the hub of the seaside entertainment industry. The use of the pier as a functional landing stage declined with the coming of the mass transport that really put the seaside resorts on the map – the railways.

The brightly painted carousel could be seen from miles away and attracted a big crowd.

The rapid expansion of the rail network during the nineteenth century brought the seaside within reach of the masses, the shorter journey times making it possible to take a day trip to the coast rather than having to book into a hotel for the night. Upper-class holidaymakers generally spent several weeks in a resort, whether following the regimes set out for them by their doctors or just enjoying the social scene: the influx of day-trippers came as something of a shock to them. Queen Victoria – and they don't come more upper class than that – decided to abandon the Royal Pavilion at Brighton when the railway arrived in 1841. She thought that the town no longer offered any privacy and was increasingly overrun with 'flashy vulgarians'. She and Prince Albert built Osborne House on the Isle of Wight as their summer retreat.

The seaside is where Britain's class system is sometimes said to have started breaking down, with people from all walks of life enjoying holidays at the same resorts. That's not entirely true. Visitors with plenty of money stayed in grand hotels, while those who didn't have so much money had to make do with a B&B if they were staying for more than a day. If a resort had more than one beach, it was more than likely that the better beach would be kept as a quieter, more refined area for the genteel holidaymaker, while the other would spawn the pubs and seafront entertainment that attracted the less refined visitor. At Blackpool, the posh people stayed away from the pier when the day-trippers were around: a second, more downmarket, pier was opened in 1868 with more entertainment and half the admission charge to lure the lower classes away from the North Pier. As visitor numbers grew, a third

Below: A right royal outing – driving the Prince of Wales past the Queen's Hotel in Llandudno.

Opposite: Well-dressed Victorian crowds on the beach at Blackpool.

10,269. - BLACKPOOL. THE TOWER WITH BEACH

pier was added to provide further entertainment for the masses in 1893, making Blackpool the only resort in Britain with three piers.

TIME OFF FOR GOOD BEHAVIOUR

There weren't only upmarket and downmarket areas in resorts – there were entire resorts that were considered a cut above their neighbours. Staying in a fashionable hotel in Cliftonville was definitely seen at one time to be more desirable than staying in rowdy Margate, even though they are right next door to each other. There was, of course, no stopping the working classes once they were given the chance to take a holiday at the seaside, and the chance was provided by the Bank Holiday Act of 1871. The Act provided for four Bank Holidays in England, Wales and Ireland giving workers the day off on Easter Monday, Whit Monday, the first Monday in August and Boxing Day (St Stephen's Day in Ireland). In Scotland the Bank Holidays were slightly different – New Year's Day, Good Friday, the first Monday in May, the first Monday in August and Christmas Day (Good Friday and Christmas Day were already holidays in the rest of Britain).

Christmas Day, Boxing Day or New Year's Day weren't the most obvious times to visit the seaside (although the original sea bathers were often winter visitors, their doctors telling them that the colder the water was, the better it was for them), but the bank holiday day-trippers soon had longer holidays to look forward to. The 'Wakes Week' started as a religious festival centuries before the Industrial Revolution, to commemorate the building of a local church or chapel, but developed into more general public celebration. In country villages, the Wakes Week was a big event because it was when the fair came to town. The fair was a livestock show and might even be a 'mop fair' when domestic and agricultural workers who were out of contract looked for new employers: a 'domestic' might carry a mop so that potential employers would immediately see what work she was used to doing; a gardener might carry a flower. They wore their best clothes in order to make a good impression, but once they were hired and had accepted a shilling or two to seal the deal, many made straight for the nearest pub.

With little or no other holidays to speak of, the workers weren't about to give up a tradition that dated back centuries just because they were moving from the land to the factory. Mill owners knew that during Wakes Week, they could expect workers to be absent, either out on drinking sprees, sleeping off hangovers or simply enjoying all the fun of the fair. Wakes Weeks became unofficial, and then official (but unpaid), holidays for factory workers across the Midlands and the North. In Glasgow, the last fortnight in July is still known as The Glasgow Fair. Mill and factory owners closed down for a week, using the time for essential repairs and maintenance, something that ever more stringent government legislation was making compulsory in any case. It wasn't until well into the twentieth century that the workers' unions were powerful enough to be able to demand holidays with pay.

Opposite: The railways offered special deals for 'Wakes Week' holidaymakers.

The pier at Llandudno
is a pretty amazing
sight from up on
the Great Orme.

Wakes Weeks had long been at different times in different areas, as the fairs travelled from town to town. This tradition continued, with towns like Bolton, Bury and Blackburn shutting down their mills on different dates to let the workers head for the coast. People saved up all year to be able to afford the family holiday, with whole streets heading off together. The factory communities were very close and people enjoyed having the comfort of their neighbours – extended families – around them when they went to the strange place on the coast. From the middle of the nineteenth century to the middle of the twentieth century, it was boom time for the British seaside. By 1911, there were around 145 major resorts around the coast of England and Wales.

WELCOME TO LLANDUDNO

The miles of sandy beaches on the Welsh coast were to provide some of the most picturesque British seaside resorts, and none more so than Llandudno. Much of Llandudno has remained unashamedly unchanged since it was first built in the 1850s and became known as the 'Queen of Welsh Resorts'. The two-mile stretch of beach that runs between its headlands – Great Orme and Little Orme – has a wide Victorian promenade that curves around the bay, with an elegant sweep of Victorian buildings following in its wake. These include the four-star St George's Hotel, the first to be built on the promenade in 1854. You might expect to see amusement arcades and gift shops squeezed in amongst the beachfront buildings – let's face it, you would in most other British resorts – but you won't find them blighting the front in Llandudno. The reason is that Mostyn Estates, which owns the land on which Llandudno is built, has been controlling all of the development here since the first brick was laid.

There was no resort at Llandudno 200 years ago. The Welsh-speaking people who lived in the area were farmers, miners and fishermen – sometimes all three. As miners, they dug not coal but the copper ore that was to be found in the limestone rock of the Great Orme. These copper mines were abandoned at the end of the Bronze Age, but reopened in the seventeenth century, with some miners still working the ore right up to the end of the nineteenth century. Until the middle of the nineteenth century there were only a few dozen cottages scattered around the Llandudno peninsula. All began to change when the most influential family in the area, the Mostyns, took over the common land in the area. In total, 832 acres were commandeered under the Inclosures Act laws, leaving just 1.5 acres to the locals. Lord Mostyn couldn't quite make up his mind what to do with all the land he had suddenly acquired. He thought about creating a commercial dock to export coal or a ferry port, but at a meeting in the King's Head inn (which is still there, opposite the Great Orme Tramway's Victoria Station) it was decided to cash in on the emerging seaside holiday fashion and build a resort.

Opposite: Who needs TV and computer games when you can have more fun riding a wooden horse?

The town was laid out as a basic grid with streets either following the line of the north shore promenade, or running away from the north shore to the sand dunes of the west shore. Many fine buildings developed over the course of the second half of the nineteenth century, including a Victorian shopping centre (or 'emporium') that would later become the Empire Hotel and, in 1877, Llandudno Pier.

Because so much of Llandudno has remained unchanged, it seemed the ideal place to go when we wanted to make a film about traditional British holidays. You can certainly find nightclubs and other modern amenities in Llandudno easily enough if you go looking for them, but the town is in no way as obviously commercialised as, for example, Blackpool. Preserving all of the older elements of the resort is, as you might expect, a never-ending task and there were plenty of jobs that I could help out with around the town.

TRAM-A-LAMA-DING-DONG!

There were a lot of things on the tramway that runs from the King's Head up the Great Orme that looked familiar to me at first glance. A railway is a railway after all, right? Wrong – the running gear and operating system on the Great Orme Tramway were nothing like the sort of thing that I had seen before on the Severn Valley line. There were wheels running on rails,

Bathing machines clutter the shoreline at Llandudno with the Great Orme and the pier in the background.

The Great Orme Tramway first opened in 1902 and was an instant success.

but that's just about where the similarities ended. For a start, this line was running up a hill steep enough to bring a smile to my face if I was coming down it on a bike. Your average railway doesn't really do that, but that is exactly why the tramway in Llandudno was built. Visitors to the resort could climb the Great Orme to enjoy the wonderful views, walking up the road to make it easier if they were reasonably fit. The steep roads, though, weren't much use to anyone who was in the least bit infirm and the solution was to build a railway that would go up the hill. They did it in San Francisco in 1873, after all, so why not in Llandudno?

The Great Orme Tramway first opened in 1902 and although it's often thought to be based on the system used in San Francisco it has far more in common with the cable haulage systems that were used in the coal mines, to bring heavily-laden wagons up to the surface. Steel cables, originally with a hemp core, ran in a slot between the tram rails that haul tram cars to the Halfway Station, which allowed the tramline to cross roads without other traffic fouling the cables. The cables then ran above ground to the terminus near the summit of the Great Orme, at 679 feet. The big difference between the Great Orme system and the San Francisco system was that in San Francisco, the cable cars detached from the cable when they needed to stop and gripped onto the moving cable when they wanted to get going again. In Llandudno the cars were permanently attached and the cable stopped and started.

The whole venture was seen as a huge gamble when the first car left the station to the sound of the town's silver band playing the national anthem, but in the first month alone the tramway carried almost 39,000 passengers, double what had been estimated. They rode in four forty-eight-seat cars, with

the cars working in pairs – the weight of one car running downhill helping to haul its partner to the top. At Halfway Station, the real power was supplied by two steam-powered winding engines, one for the upper section and one for the lower. Passengers change cars here for the upper leg of the journey. It can get quite blustery and, as there's no glass in the tramcar windows, you sometimes have to hold on to your hat.

The tramway still looks pretty much as it did over a hundred years ago, thanks to the skills of the people who keep it in top condition. There have, though, been a number of significant changes. The steam engines were replaced by electric motors in 1957, still at a time when most railway locomotives were steam powered, although the steam engines' fifty-five years' service is pretty good going by anyone's standards. The original overhead copper wire that controlled the bell and telephone communications between the driver and the winding engineer is now a state-of-the-art underground electronic system, showing the engineer exactly where each of the cars is on a video display. The brakes and safety systems are also much improved on the originals. Even so, the Victorians who built the tramway would still recognise their handiwork. Though they might have heart attacks if they saw the £4 million bill for the tramway's centenary restoration, especially given that they only paid £20,000 to build it in the first place ...

THE PLEASURES OF A PLEASURE PIER

Something that has changed a fair bit since it was first built is Llandudno Pier. The pier is at the foot of the Great Orme on the north shore and reaches out over 2,295 feet into the Irish Sea, making it the longest pier in Wales and the fifth longest in Britain. There has been a pier of some sort at Llandudno since 1858, although that original wooden pier was less than 250 feet long and was destroyed by a storm only a year after it opened. It was rebuilt and used as a landing stage for steam ships, but as the town had its own railway station by 1858, the pier wasn't quite so important for bringing visitors into the resort. Even after the current pier was built, however, it continued to be used as a landing stage, most recently for pleasure cruises.

The present pier was begun in September 1876, designed by Scottish engineer Sir James Brunlees and built by Walter Macfarlane of Glasgow: Macfarlane used decorative cast iron from another Glasgow manufacturer, the Elmbank Foundry. Originally the pier entrance was at 'Happy Valley' at the foot of the Great Orme, but it was extended to provide another entrance closer to the promenade in 1884. It opened to the public in August, 1877 and has always been primarily a pleasure pier.

When the railways became the most popular mode of transport for everyone heading to the seaside, piers that had been landing stages for steamers quickly found a new function as pleasure piers. Holidaymakers enjoyed, and still enjoy, being able to walk out over the water and look back at the town to

Above opposite: When you have your own carousel, it's not difficult to attract the ladies.

Below opposite: Everyone wanted to take a spin, young and not-so-young . . .

take in a view of the resort, as opposed to their more usual view out to sea. While taking a gentle stroll along the flat wooden deck of the pier, they were, inevitably, tempted to part with some of their holiday money at stalls and kiosks set up on the pier. Just as the pier was an extension of the resort's promenade, so the pier vendors provided an extension of the town's shops and entertainments.

By 1894, you might have been tempted to buy a postcard on the pier to send home, using the new halfpenny adhesive stamps that pretty much guaranteed next-day delivery now that the railways could transport the Royal Mail so effectively. The postcard would have been pretty plain, though – probably without even an illustration. What we would recognise as a postcard nowadays, something printed with an illustration or photograph of Llandudno, didn't come along until around 1902. This was when the postcard really started to become part of the seaside holiday tradition. Comic postcards – the fat lass on the beach, the henpecked husband or the honeymoon couple – featuring saucy cartoons didn't really appear until the 1920s and 1930s, but there were other things on the pier that reflected the slightly 'naughty' atmosphere at the seaside.

Drop a coin in a slot and crank the handle on a Mutoscope and you could see 'What The Butler Saw' – a through-the-keyhole moving image of 'M'lady' disrobing to step into a bath or go to bed. The Mutoscope worked like a 'flip book', turning over a series of images illuminated by a lightbulb inside the machine and viewed through an eyepiece. From the time these machines first began to appear in the late 1890s, they became hugely popular, but were denounced in a letter to *The Times* in 1899 as 'vicious demoralising picture shows', contributing to 'the corruption of the young that comes from exhibiting under a strong light, nude female figures'. It's quite surprising that the machines weren't banned completely given Victorian attitudes to proper dress and behaviour in public, but they survived along with a host of other coin-operated machines that would tell your fortune, test your strength, weigh you, measure you or even give you an electric shock (which was thought to be very therapeutic).

Entertainment on the piers of Britain was not only by machine, though. Once you had taken a stroll out to the end of the pier, you would be able to sit for a while and listen to a band play at a bandstand or in a pavilion. The Llandudno pier's sundeck pavilion at the end of the pier was so popular that they needed somewhere bigger to stage musical shows. In 1881, the Llandudno Pier Company decided to build a 2,000-seat venue at the shore end of the pier. It was three storeys high, had a beautifully detailed cast-iron veranda facing out to sea and in its basement boasted the largest indoor swimming pool in Britain. The Pier Pavilion Theatre opened in 1886 and, although there were water quality problems with the swimming pool that led to it being filled in, it remained as an entertainment venue into the 1980s, with top acts such

The 'What The Butler Saw' risqué entertainment machines first began to appear in the 1890s.

as George Formby, Ted Ray, Petula Clark and Cliff Richard including the theatre on their tour schedules. Sadly, the pavilion closed in 1990 and was destroyed by a fire in 1994.

TIME TO GET STUCK IN...

The pier, of course, survived and I was lucky enough to be allowed to help out with some essential restoration work. Of all the jobs that I tackled during the making of the TV series, this was the one that I enjoyed the most – and it takes some doing to beat driving a steam locomotive, let me tell you. It wasn't just that it was interesting work, there was also a real element of danger involved and, if you hadn't already guessed, I am a bit of an adrenalin junkie. The guys that I worked with were proper grafters. Their attitude reminded me of the stories about the navvies: the blokes working on the pier restoration

After getting all togged up in safety gear, I began to wonder what I had let myself in for . . .

loved their ale, and they stayed out till all hours downing pint after pint. That's not something I can cope with – one sniff of the barmaid's apron and I've had it. But these lads were there ready for work at the crack of dawn to make the most of all the daylight they could get.

The job that I was able to help with involved replacing the cross-members that braced the legs of the pier. Naturally, the bolts that had originally been used to hold them in place had long since rusted solid. There was no way you could ever hope to move them with a drop of release oil and a spanner. They had to be cut off using oxyacetylene torches. The only way to get to them was to climb down from the pier itself. We had all the right sort of safety equipment – hard hats, gloves, masks and, most importantly, safety harnesses. To begin with, the lads wouldn't even let me clip my own safety line on and off. They might act a bit rough, but they've got a proper respect for their job. It's not just the height we were working at that made it dangerous: you're also working in a constant breeze or even a strongish wind (too strong and you're hauled out of there); then there's the tide either coming in or going out, waves lashing against the legs of the pier making everything wet and slippery. That's no joke when you're trying to find a good, solid foothold so that you can brace yourself properly in order to hit the spot with a cutting torch that burns at 3,500 degrees Celsius.

I'm no stranger to using a welding torch, but dangling underneath Llandudno Pier gave me a whole new respect for the thing. The last thing you want to do under those circumstances is to slip slightly and drag that flame across your leg. As it was, when the flame hit the flaky rust it sent sparks flying everywhere. Most of these cool off almost instantly but a few fly free, burning red hot for a couple of seconds. I had a proper hot rust flake spark off and shoot down the top of my boiler suit – that left a scorch mark in a very tender place! That night we went to the King's Head for dinner (they do fantastic speciality pies) and took part in the pub quiz. In my honour, the TV crew named our team 'Burnt Nipple'!

SWIMMING LESSONS

I like to think that we did our bit to uphold the seaside's saucy reputation there, though that sort of thing would have been frowned upon by the Victorians. They preferred that, in public, there should be no mention of anything of a sexual nature and body parts had to be kept strictly under wraps. In the early nineteenth century, it was common for men and boys who went swimming in the sea, lakes or rivers to jump in naked. Not that many people actually went swimming as very few, including most sailors, knew how to swim. But by the middle of the nineteenth century, it was illegal to swim nude. Men had to wear swimming drawers that, once they were wet, tended to fall down. These evolved into a swimsuit that was like a t-shirt with a pair of shorts attached. Ladies' swimwear, meanwhile, covered them even more. By the end of the nineteenth century, they were wearing long bathing dresses that had weights in the hems to stop the dress rising up in the water.

Even then, no one actually saw them wearing the things as they went into the water with the aid of a bathing machine. This was a sort of shed on wheels that was pushed out into the water, once the lady inside had changed out of her day wear and into her swimming gown. She then emerged from the bathing machine's seaward door where a canvas awning was lowered so that she could take a dip without anyone seeing her. Even then, ladies would have their own stretch of beach and men swimming within 200 yards of the ladies' area could be fined.

Quite often, the lady bather would be aided by a female 'dipper', usually one of the family who ran the bathing machines franchise, who would dunk her in the water, holding her under for as many seconds as the doctor had prescribed. Eventually, the 'dippers' became swimming instructors and the ladies' costumes became a bit more manageable, but it wasn't until the 1920s that ladies started to wear one-piece swimsuits that actually allowed them to swim.

> ... but working underneath the pier was a fantastic job to do.

At the beginning of the twentieth century, the beach at Llandudno was lined with bathing machines, but because these were quite expensive to rent, they were something for the more affluent beachgoer. Those on a more limited budget simply would not go into the water. The rules about separate sections of beach for males and females were relaxed by the start of the twentieth century and families could spend time together on the beach, although it was generally only children who were dressed in swimsuits. Mum and Dad, right up to the 1950s, would remain fully dressed, with Dad in a suit, shirt and tie. If it was really hot, he might take off his jacket but the tie would most likely remain tied. This was partly a throwback to Victorian attitudes, which had developed not only because it was felt improper to show any naked flesh, but also because it was not fashionable to be suntanned. Only those who worked in the fields exposed themselves to the sun, after all. Having pale skin let everyone know that you didn't have to work outdoors. They didn't, at that time, know anything about the dangers of overexposure to strong sunlight.

THAT'S THE WAY TO DO IT

There was, in any case, always more to do at the seaside than lounging on the beach. At Llandudno, on the promenade near the pier, there was, and still is, Professor Codman's Punch and Judy Show. The Professor (and his descendants who still run the show) has been there since he was given special permission by Lord Mostyn to set up his show on the promenade in 1864. Punch and Judy was already a well-established tradition in Britain by that time. The character had started life in Italy in the sixteenth century and was introduced to Britain by an Italian puppet showman in 1662. Professor Codman, who had been a travelling actor, and his wife decided to make their home in Llandudno in 1860. He used scavenged driftwood to carve their Punch and Judy puppets – the family is still using those puppets today. Punch and Judy has become such an integral part of the seaside tradition that Professor Codman's show remains the only entertainment of its kind that is permitted on the promenade at Llandudno.

This presented something of a problem when we were filming the TV show, because we wanted to show a traditional Victorian helter skelter and fairground carousel with the beach and the sea on one side and the beautiful Victorian buildings along the promenade on the other. We were given special permission to set up on the promenade and I know that people who love Llandudno and go back year after year weren't best pleased about seeing the fairground attractions there – I hope they took some photos because they're not very likely ever to see them there again. You might see them in Mostyn Street, which runs parallel to the promenade a couple of streets back from the sea front, as they have a three-day Victorian funfair every year over the May Day bank holiday weekend. And you can't have a funfair without a helter skelter.

The bathing machine was still in use right up to the early part of the twentieth century, although by then ladies' bathing costumes had become far more practical.

The helter skelter
looked quite sad
without its top.

ALL THE FUN OF (BUILDING) THE FAIR

The first helter skelters may well have been built in America, where they are sometimes called 'tornado slides', but by the early 1900s they were all the rage at British seaside resorts. The one that I helped to put together on the promenade at Llandudno was about fifty feet high. You can tell why they liked to build them at the end of a pier – people would be able to see them for miles, especially at night when the cabin at the top was lit up. They were often called 'lighthouse slips' for obvious reasons.

Our helter skelter was a piece of joinery that my mate Mave would have been proud of. Basically, it was built using a series of wooden panels on frames – a bit like fence panels. But these panels wouldn't be any good for fencing in your garden. Each one is specially shaped to create the tapered hexagon shape of the helter skelter structure. The panels also have special fittings attached at exactly the right place, to help support the slide that spirals round the outside and the staircase that spirals up the inside. They have to go together in a certain sequence and are all numbered on the inside. Unfortunately, because the whole thing had just been lovingly restored and repainted, the numbers were missing – they'd been painted over. That didn't put the guys who own the helter skelter off for long. They know the thing so well that they were able crack on with bolting it all together.

Professor Codman's Punch and Judy show.

There was no crane or hoist used in assembling the helter skelter – it all went together using muscle power. At first, I couldn't figure out why, when there was a perfectly good staircase inside, we were marching up the slippery chute on the outside. Space on the inside is limited, though, and carrying bulky panels and roof sections up the tower is easier if you can allow bits of them to overhang out into clear space on the outside of the slip. You need good grips on the soles of your boots when you're carrying a load up a helter skelter slide, and a fair amount of stamina as well. It was all worth it, however, by the time I was able to hoist the Union Jack on the roof at the very top. We then had to try the helter skelter out, sliding down the

The lack of room to manoeuvre on the staircase inside meant that the big panels had to be carried up the slide on the outside.

slip sitting on cork mats. I went down with a cameraman in tow and, even though we didn't get up that much speed, I could see why the Victorians and Edwardians thought they were so much fun.

The name 'helter skelter' comes from a term that has been around for centuries and means 'in chaotic and disorderly haste'. Helter skelter is what they call a rhyming duplication, like 'pell mell' or 'hodge podge'. Our second run on the slip was done with far more disorderly haste and we landed at the bottom in fits of giggles to find that there was already a queue of kids forming, who wanted to have a go. One little girl dragged her mum up to the top three times and then made her dad take her up again twice! A lovely old lady, aged ninety-two, stopped, took a look at the blue-and-white tower and said, 'I haven't been on one of those since I were a lass . . .' It seems the helter skelter appeals to young and old alike. The old lady decided against giving it a go, though.

Next to our lighthouse slip was a truly breathtaking 1882 carousel. It was everything you would expect a fairground ride to be, painted in bright colours, sparkling with mirrors and throbbing with music from its organ pipes. What's more, it was all powered by steam. There was a mighty great traction engine parked alongside it, but that wasn't what was supplying the

Almost finished – just waiting for me to hoist the Union Jack on top.

Now we were able
to enjoy all the fun
of the fair in the
Welsh sunshine.

Above: The kids who gathered round the helter skelter found my test run highly amusing.

Opposite: Preparing for my musical debut with the band on the seafront.

power. The carousel had its own steam engine in the middle of the ride that drove the roundabout and lifted its 'gallopers', which is what the whole ride is often called, up and down the country. The traction engine, a brightly painted 'showman's engine', was there to provide electricity.

I was feeling like something of an old hand with traction engines by now and was given the chance to drive this one along the promenade. I had to take it easy, mind you, because all these machines have their own little foibles and this one, called the *Prince of Wales,* was no exception. It was originally intended for military use, one of several engines that were built for export to Russia where they were intended to be used to haul artillery. No one's entirely sure why they were never shipped to Russia but I think the date on the side of the *Prince* probably has something to do with it – 1917. That's when the Russians were having their revolution, so maybe it wasn't the best time to be shipping expensive machinery there – not if you wanted to get paid for it at any rate! The *Prince* was used as an agricultural engine for a while and then, quite bizarrely, in the 1950s, when most other showman's engines were being scrapped, the *Prince* was converted into just that.

The number of cheap, ex-army trucks available just after the Second World War made steam transport a thing of the past on the roads, but in the nineteenth century and the early part of the twentieth century, the powerful showman's engine – perhaps more properly called a road locomotive – would have towed the wagons that carried the disassembled fairground rides from

town to town. It did the job of a whole team of horses, but it was also part of the show itself. The showman's engine was more brightly painted than most other working engines, making it a sight to behold as it came trundling into town. When it was new, the *Prince* would have cost around 2,000 guineas (a guinea being twenty-one shillings as opposed to the twenty shillings in a pound) at a time when most people were earning less than £1 a week. It was an expensive investment for the showman, but some manufacturers offered the opportunity to pay by instalments to ease the pain.

The *Prince's* job on the promenade at Llandudno was to provide electric power for the ride's lights. Some showman's engines had cranes attached to help assemble the rides, but almost all had dynamos or generators that provided electric power to light the hundreds of bulbs on the fairground rides. The bright lights of the fairground would have been a revelation to most ordinary people in the early 1900s as they wouldn't have electric light in their own homes. I was shown how to loop a drive belt around the flywheel that was turned by the *Prince's* royal steam power, with the belt providing power to the generator. A cable then ran from the generator that sat on top of the front end of the boiler to the gallopers.

We had two sets of gallopers on the promenade. The larger one provided the traditional fairground organ music, courtesy of a restored, steam-powered organ that was originally made in France (as most of these organs were). The ride's horses were carved to a set pattern but all painted differently and individually named. Traditionally, the horses round the outside are named after the owner's immediate family, with more distant family names used as you go in towards the middle. They were all looking immaculate and as soon as the ride started turning and the music started playing, it attracted Llandudno's promenaders like bees around a honey pot. When we wanted to film people enjoying the ride, it didn't take much to persuade riders of all ages to hop aboard.

The other carousel was a much smaller, hand-cranked affair. I had a go at winding the handle and it was surprisingly easy once you got the thing going. I had to take it easy once we got up a bit of speed, though, otherwise we would have had children flying off in all directions! At one time most fairground gallopers – also known as 'dobbies' – used people power. The owners would even get children who couldn't afford the halfpenny fair to crank the handle that turned the ride, or simply push the roundabout so that others could enjoy the ride. Eventually, they would earn the chance to have a ride themselves. Real horses were also used alongside the wooden ones and the larger of the Llandudno rides had an area of the deck where there were seats rather than gallopers. That area had once been where the animal horsepower plodded round before the ride was converted to steam horsepower.

Opposite: All that practice with two spanners and an old bucket was well worthwhile.

Maintaining and upgrading the rides was a constant expense for the showman and buying a new ride cost an absolute fortune. A hundred years ago a switchback ride – a carousel where the deck moved up and down and the carriages might spin, as on the famous 'waltzers' – could cost as much as £30,000. That really was a hefty amount to pay out back then and probably compares with thrill-seekers at funfairs nowadays strapping themselves into rides that have cost over £1.7 million – all the fun of the fair has never come cheap.

FINISHING WITH A BANG

The last job I had to do in Llandudno wasn't what you would call dangerous. There was no fear for life and limb like dangling over the side of the pier with a cutting torch – but it was a nerve-racking task all the same. I had to get dressed up in a bandsman's uniform to play timpani with a band on the promenade bandstand to entertain those out for an early evening stroll. Anyone who spotted a madman up on the Great Orme earlier that day pounding out a rhythm on an upturned bucket with a couple of spanners knows how much effort I put into making sure that I didn't let down the rest of the lads in the band. I think it went okay in the end.

The best thing about playing with the band was that we were facing in towards the hotels that look out across the promenade. Apart from the cars parked in the street, it was pretty much the same view that a Victorian holidaymaker would have seen. The Mostyn Estates and the local authorities have done a grand job in preserving the resort and although it has grown a fair bit since Queen Elizabeth of Roumania had a five-week stay here in 1890, calling Llandudno 'a beautiful haven of peace' (later adopted as the town's motto), Her Majesty would most certainly still recognise the place. The fact that it has not been turned into an inferno of neon lights definitely appeals to those who come back here year after year. We filmed there in March, not during a traditional holiday period or school holidays, yet finding hotel rooms wasn't easy as they were all booked up.

The jet age may have turned every corner of the world into extra optional stops on an extended Grand Tour, tempting Brits to holiday abroad, but the good old British seaside holiday still survives and, in Llandudno, is surviving in style.

This was a pretty good way to finish off a great visit to the seaside at Llandudno.

ACKNOWLEDGEMENTS

From North One Television I would like to thank
Neil Duncanson, James Woodroffe and Ewan Keil.

Thank you to all of the volunteers and workers at:
Severn Valley Railway, Gayle Mill, Brixham Harbour and
Trinity Sailing, The Birmingham Botanical Gardens
and Rock & Water, The Black Country Living Museum and
GW Conservation, Llandudno Pier and the Great Orme
Tramway and everyone who generously gave their time
to help make the show.

Finally, I would like to thank the original eighteenth-
and nineteenth-century workers who grafted so we
had something to film!

PICTURE CREDITS

INDEX